THE JOSHUA FACTOR

David —
with thanks for your leadership in
Chicago + Blackhawk + Joy in
your friendship.
Thanks for all you do +
who you are
in Christ

THE JOSHUA FACTOR

Leadership Principles from an

Ancient Warrior

Jonathan B. Krogh

Library of Congress Control Number:		2009907063
ISBN:	Hardcover	978-1-4415-5541-0
	Softcover	978-1-4415-5540-3

Cover art by French painter Nicholas Poussin, JOSHUA FIGHTS AMALEK, ca. 1625, oil on canvas, 97 × 134 cm, ca. 1625, The Hermitage, St. Petersburg.

Unless otherwise noted, scripture references are taken from the HOLY BIBLE, NEW INTERNATIONAL VERSION®, Copyright ©1973, 1978, 1984 International Bible Society. All rights reserved.

This book was printed in the United States of America.

To order additional copies of this book, contact:
Xlibris Corporation
1-888-795-4274
www.Xlibris.com
Orders@Xlibris.com
57969

In memory of my father,
Oakley M. Krogh,
a Joshua leader.

Acknowledgments

A first attempt such as this does not happen in a vacuum. There are many whom I wish to thank for their inspiration and encouragement in completing this book.

I would also like to specifically express my appreciation to those who added their editorial eyes, including my life-long friend John Carlson, my sisters Linda Spencer and Jill Rebbeck, and my ministerial colleagues The Reverend R. Milton Winter, The Reverend Timothy J. Mitchell, and Chaplain Dan Swets. In addition I want to thank Professor Paul E. Capetz for assisting with early stylistic comments, and reminding me to carefully avoid the split infinitive. Also thanks to the Reverend Kyle M. Roggenbuck for her willingness to undertake final edits.

I also wish to express my deep gratitude to Dani for her continuing encouragement and patience as I "rambled" these concepts into a finished manuscript.

Love to my son Calvin for tolerating his father throughout this project and for sharing the computer.

Lastly I wish to thank the members and leaders of the many congregations and ministries of which I have been a part. Your grace in receiving my presence and service has given substance to this book. What I have received from your fellowship and wisdom far exceeds anything I have given.

Jonathan B. Krogh
July 2009

CONTENTS

INTRODUCTION

T his book is written to inspire the Joshuas among us. Pastors and congregational leaders who, when they lack formal authority have the patience to endure stagnation; but when given the opportunity to lead, they push beyond personal anxiety moving relentlessly toward what is promised.

How do you know if you're a Joshua leader? Consider the following "Joshua Leader" test questions:

- Are you accused of being a "non-team-player" when you appeal to your congregation's mission?
- Are you dismissed as obsessive compulsive when you demand accountability from yourself, and foolishly naive when you expect accountability from others?
- Do you chafe when those in charge reject proposals in the name of caution?
- Are you accused of being callous or unsympathetic because you give little attention to complainers?
- Do you believe change only arises from the hard work of discipline coupled with a dedication to integrity?
- Are you accused of being picky because you insist upon accurate and consistent documentation?
- Do you keep your word even when others tell you it isn't worth it?
- Do you believe problem solving is more important than blame?

If you answered "yes" to some or all of these questions, you may be a Joshua leader.

Many who hold responsibility for communities of faith feel their abilities constrained by the keepers of "conventional" wisdom. Joshua leaders understand the need for caution but have a driving passion to move beyond it. Ignoring the advice of the majority, they often suggest taking on the "giants" against impossible odds. And while Joshua leaders may understand the organization's mission better than those in charge, if they aren't careful, they will find themselves fired for "irritating" the *status quo*.

Some may find this book lacking in the "how-to" department. If you are looking for a method or technique don't bother reading further. This book is about the identity and character of powerful leaders, not formulae for success. Packaged programs are for those who are more comfortable following instructions than plotting a course. Joshua leaders have an oriented vision continually expressed through effective administration. They understand that relentless administration, not visionary ideas, transform communities.

When it comes to the church I believe administration is practically sacramental. It may seem odd to use the character of a Biblical warrior to inspire better budgets, faithful stewardship, and productive committees, but I am convinced administration will determine the future of the modern Christian church.

From the Latin *administro,* administration means to guide, wait upon, or to serve. The activity of administration is very close in meaning to the Greek word from which we derive the title *deacon.* Deacons were the first Church administrators called to oversee the contribution, meal preparation, and hands-on ministry of the Jerusalem congregation. The position of deacon was necessitated by ethnic tension in the first generation Christian Church (Acts 6:1-6) and it was a church administrator, Stephen, who was the first martyr of the Christian Church (Acts 7:54-60).

The verb *administer* is used to describe both the analysis of an organization's budget (as in the *administration* of business), and the distribution of the church's sacraments (as in the *administration* of the Eucharist). That is how it should be.

Faithful congregational administration permits a real-world context for the proclamation of the Word and distribution of the Sacraments. Poor management has a direct and withering impact on the community's ability to demonstrate the evidence of God's grace. If the corporate institution is hobbled, the spiritual opportunity is lost. As every congregation hears in stewardship sermons, being faithful to baptismal vows requires faithful management of the community's institutional resources. Without proper administration of the institution, the administration of the sacraments becomes impracticable.

Unfortunately, too many pastors are quick to dismiss the responsibility of administration as somehow "too secular" for their hands or "too tedious" for their dispositions. And while some individuals may not possess the constitution to accomplish specific administrative tasks, dismissing administration's importance undermines mission. Without effective corporate administration, the holy expression of Divine ministry falls into deficit.

To administer with discipline and integrity is to *minister*. Clear, commonly shared, open processes permit the congregation to accomplish acts of compassion, but without these processes, liturgy—'the work of the people'—is corruptible and ineffectual. Far too often popular leaders construct quick empires, only to have them crumble because of their inability to give an accounting for their work. The timeless enduring work of the community can only take root when the means and processes by which they grow are open and accountable. *Part of every great idea should be the capacity for it to survive an audit.*

By administration I mean not only the organizational charts and financial accounting of the congregation, but also the constitution, bylaws, and minutes of the organization's proceedings. Far too often church leaders dismiss the work of documentation and recording as intrusions into the creative functioning of their organizations. Some leaders perceive even polity as something to be circumvented when a particular idea warrants an "end-run" around a more accountable process. But leaders adopt such thinking to their peril, not only because they may be audited by the state or reviewed by a denominational committee, but because good process only confirms good ideas.

What's more, like procedures required for a science-fair project, effective processes allow good ideas to be both revisable and repeatable. Failure to maintain even the most rudimentary form of documentation makes it impossible for the community to recall its road to success or backtrack from a dead-end. Without effective documentation, organizations tend to repeat themselves. Unfortunately, they most frequently repeat their mistakes.

Simply stated, effective administration makes the work of the congregation possible. And while adherence to process for its own sake occasionally slows creativity, I know of no congregation that has closed its doors because it spent too much time and energy keeping accurate records and ensuring due process. Quite the contrary, when reviewing the most difficult and destructive periods of a congregation's history (those when there was scandal or division), one usually finds the poorest record keeping (incomplete minutes, inaccurate rolls, unrecorded certificates, etc.).

This book is not about individual hearts, although they are always at stake. This book is about the moving of the Spirit among the shared community of faith. To speak of the Church we must speak of *congregations* for they are the most basic and concrete building blocks of the greater Church.

I concur with my own denomination's expression, that the full Church of Jesus Christ is a much larger and more mystical interconnection of these local units.

We affirm that the several different congregations of believers, taken collectively, constitute one Church of

—

Christ, called emphatically *the Church* (italics mine).
[Presbyterian Church USA Book of Order G-1.0400]

I wish to be clear, I am writing for congregations, by which I mean a gathering of people who have united and incorporated as a 501-c3 organization for religious purposes. While there may be expressions of Divine possibility in their midst, these possibilities are expressed in very human form. Budgets, balance sheets, and bylaws constitute these human organizations, and these corporate elements articulate institutional success or failure. But these elements alone should not be confused with the affirmation of God's blessing or validation of human effort.

Congregations flush with members, programs, and new construction must not be mistaken for a people who are spiritually grounded and faithfully interconnected. Accountability, not accumulation, confirms faithfulness.

If there is a future for the Church, it will unfold from local congregations. Not that ecumenical conferences, denominational assemblies, judicatories, or dioceses have no purpose; they most certainly do. But as life is made possible by the absorption of nutrients and the dispelling of waste on the cellular level, so too the Church finds its expression of vitality or evidence of decay in the smallest expression of its being—the congregation.

Some may balk at the metaphor and suggest the smallest measure of the church is the individual soul finding his or her life and redemption through a one-on-one relationship with God through a personal affirmation of faith in Christ. While I agree one's private spiritual formation is important, such formation should not be confused with the *body* of Christ. That is the Church! And the clearest flesh and blood manifestation of that body is each and every Christian congregation.

"All politics is local!" once declared Speaker of the House, Tip O'Neil. The same should be said of Christian religion. Private faith is a matter of *credo*, but what follows the "I believe" only has content as real flesh and blood communities articulate, nurture, and live their faith in the particular and unique location of the congregation.

What follows is intended for "formal" congregational leaders. By formal leaders I mean those who are selected, ordained, installed, or commissioned to direct the congregation's institutional and spiritual life. I write to leaders because they are the ones given the responsibility and to whom members and non-members alike turn for guidance. Formal church leaders are endowed by the community with certain responsibilities. Failure to undertake these responsibilities faithfully, trivializes the historic authority of office and thereby dismisses the "official" character of the Church.

To blame the Church's shortcomings on culture, neighborhoods, politics, or denominations is to claim that health and vitality fall from above like so much *manna*, imagining that the only hope for survival comes from institutional forces beyond our control. But in the wilderness *manna* was a question—*what is it?* And without leaders on the ground telling the people to gather it up and eat, the people will starve.

Congregational leaders are those who identify the "stuff" lying around. They tell the people if it is food or poison. It is the responsibility of leaders to comprehend the difference. They serve as the "field-guides" who know the produce and the process. Leaders must first see and understand what surrounds them; they must know how to gather it; and how to use it for the nourishment of the congregation. Likewise they must also know what should be avoided and warn the congregation of what may be toxic. Congregational leaders take their members to the food God has provided, and show by example, discipline, and integrity how and where sustenance may be found.

As a pastor and a consultant I have come to believe every congregation has a lot of *manna* lying around. Sadly, many resources remain unrecognized by the leaders, and so remain unclaimed by the people. What you have in abundance, God has given and whatever God has given, true leaders will use for good purpose.

Unfortunately many leaders tend to be more attentive to what might be toxic rather than what is nourishing. When pastoral candidates interview with a prospective congregation, a majority of the questions focus on pathology: *"What keeps this congregation from growing? Where's the conflict? Whom should I watch out for? Where can we get more money?"* Little attention is given to possibility. *"What does this church do really well? What gifts and abilities do the members possess? What are the secrets of your success?"* Shifting attention from pathogen to possibility transforms ministry.

Colleagues have often told me the future of their congregation is closure. Occasionally new pastors are informed by judicatories that their congregation is dying and most likely won't make it. Seldom have I had a colleague tell me, "The judicatory told me my congregation is about to explode in membership and I am simply told not to screw it up." Or, "You know they don't see it yet, but my congregation is poised to expand mission in ways never dreamed possible!"

Leaders distracted by problems are, of course, safer. If every congregation sees nothing more than decline courting disaster, then when things turn out poorly there are no surprises—nobody gets blamed. If you call everything "poison", you'll never die of poisoning; but on the other hand, you will starve.

Like the children of Israel receiving the report of the twelve spies in the desert of Paran, most congregations never enter the fight. They delight in the fact they have never lost a battle, but then again, they never leave the wilderness.

I write for formal congregational leaders because they are the ones called upon to be responsible and, in order to fulfill their calling, they must be discerning and decisive.

The principles in this book have implications for any leader regardless of context. (If you find the book too religious, merely substitute the word "business" for "congregation" and "CEO" for "pastor".) As for my extensive use of scripture, it is important to remember these texts are *histories* documenting the military, political, and social decisions, and delineating the consequences of those decisions on the lives of real people. As leaders in an all-too-human context, I believe the successes and failures recorded in Biblical stories have much to teach us.

This book is divided into two parts each expressing a distinct dimension of congregational leadership. The first section analyzes Joshua's administrative style in stark contrast to the administrative style of Moses. Joshua held very specific values which oriented his leadership. These values included his approach to change, his commitment to discipline, and his unwavering integrity. Underlying Part I is a theoretical analysis of Joshua's attributes as a leader.

Part II divides Joshua's final lecture (Joshua 24) into eight parts. In this speech Joshua leaves for his congregation, and for us, a straight-forward outline of eight principles for effective administration. These components affect committees and congregational meetings, budgets and accounting, records and reviews. Not the kind of stuff one would associate with a great warrior, but keys to Joshua's success.

If you are looking for a direct application of Joshua's leadership principles without wading through the analysis, you may wish to begin by reading Part II.

Like Joshua's creating and developing the identity of a nation, those who administer congregations must clearly express their Christian identity. In Eucharistic liturgy *and* committee minutes, baptismal font *and* balance ledger, congregational leaders proclaim, refine, and live-out the expression of God's people.

Two score years after meeting God in the smoke of Mount Sinai, Moses dies; and 33 days later Joshua leads the people across the Jordan to the land they had only sung about for a generation. What inspired the writing of this book was a single burning question. Why after forty years in the wilderness were the people able to enter the Promised Land under Joshua when they could not under Moses?

Something changed between the death of Moses and the command of Joshua. That something was leadership.

PART I

A WARRIOR'S LEADERSHIP

Chapter I

Moses: The Cost of Reluctance

J oshua. The name bespeaks strength, confidence, and authority.

Joshua, the son of Nun, the steely-eyed warrior of the Canaanite conquest, possessed an uncanny ability to speak honestly, build loyalty, and command to victory.

Joshua, the one who "fit the battle", was an uncompromising leader both on and off the battlefield.

His given name was Hoshea, meaning "one who saves", but Moses tweaked Hoshea's name, by adding the divine prefix "JO" (short for Jehovah) naming salvation's source.

"Jehovah Saves" became his name, transforming his title from generic salvation to the declaration of God's specific intervention (Numbers 13:16).

Every time the people called out "Joshua" they invoked God's salvation, and under this name a wandering people fought their way home into the living affirmation of God's promise.

But for most of his career, Joshua was the patient third in command.

Early on, Joshua had been recognized for his leadership ability. His first major assignment came soon after the Exodus. When the people needed a general to respond to the advancement of Amalek in the valley of Rephidim (Exodus 17:8), Joshua was the only name on Moses' lips. Something about this tribal commander from Ephraim inspired the troops, making conscription easy and retreat unthinkable.

The Egyptian army had been defeated at the crossing of the Red Sea, but that victory was God's doing; the people were only observers. At Raphidim the Israelite army faced their first battle-test. Victory was crucial if these runaways were to gain the confidence necessary to become a nation.

Moses moved to high ground to witness the conflict. He held his arms over the battlefield and watched the inexperienced refugees of Israel rout the nomadic warriors of the Amalekites. So inspiring was Joshua's command that Moses recorded the details of the victory in his journal and read the entry repeatedly in front of Joshua and his men. Recounting the victory confirmed Moses' confidence and Joshua's competence (Exodus 17:10-14).

But Raphidim was the first and only victory for the next 38 years, and one of only a handful of military victories Moses would witness.[1]

Even though Moses often sang the praises of Joshua's military genius in defeating the far more experienced Amalekites, such laud resulted in no promotion. Joshua remained a military assistant, third in command behind Moses the prince, and Aaron the priest. We have no record of Joshua's attitude regarding his position in the wilderness. Unlike other characters given to complaint, Joshua remained quiet.

When Moses needed a valet to accompany him to Mt. Sinai, he left Aaron in charge of the people and tapped Joshua to be his companion. Leaving the people with instructions to wait, Moses ascended the Mountain with Joshua. On the final assent Joshua remained at base-camp waiting the return of the great liberator (Exodus 24:13-14).

When the council of the seventy was appointed to adjudicate the disputes of the people, Joshua was the only one who warned Moses of the failure to observe due process (Numbers 11:24-30).

When Moses needed spies to check out their inheritance, Joshua made the cut to the final twelve (Numbers 13:8), and was one of only two spies who believed the Covenant was greater than the giants (Numbers 14:6-9).

But Joshua's words were ignored to the peril of the people. He remained without the authority to lead for the next three and a half decades. Moses was in

---

[1] Moses did not see military victory again until after the death of Aaron when the king of Arad ambushed the people on the road to Athraim. They defeated the army of Arad and released those taken hostage; and renamed the land Hormah (*land of destruction*) (Numbers 21:1-3). Towards the end of Moses' life, there were two defensive victories. The first occurred as the people moved northeast through the desert of Kedemoth and away from their nearly four decades of wandering, and Moses attempted a treaty with Sihon king of Heshbon (the land near Mt. Nebo). Sihon rejected the offer and was defeated in the battle at Jahaz (Deuteronomy 2:26-37). Not long after that victory, Og the king of Bashan (a territory well to the northeast of where the people were planning to travel) attacked the Israelites, who defeated them, destroying all sixty cities of Og all the way to Edrei several miles north and east of where they would later cross the Jordan River (Deuteronomy 3:1-11).

charge, they would not leave the wilderness as long as Moses was alive. Like so many congregations with qualified but unused leaders, they were stuck. Joshua was stuck . . . waiting.

Between the end of Moses' career, in the 34th chapter of Deuteronomy, and the beginning of Joshua's leadership, in the 1st chapter of Joshua, little had changed. The congregation was still the same slave-descended nomads; they had the same untested army, the same law, same personnel, same training, identical resources and infrastructure. The transformation that made conquest possible was not a shift in people or program; the biggest change was the shift from Moses to Joshua.

Moses is among the most significant religious figures in human history. He was the great law-giver and the one who negotiated the liberation of the children of Israel from the hand of the oppressor. His tenure of leadership transformed, one might even say *created*, the identity of an entire nation and defined forever the notion of civil code and religious law.

But despite all of his famed qualities, Moses was unfit to lead the children of Israel into the Land of Promise. Or more to the point, something about Joshua made him *more* fit to lead the people across the Jordan.

Moses was the lone baby boy to survive the purge of the Hebrews by a paranoid Egyptian Pharaoh. Troubled by the edict that all Hebrew male children under the age of two were to be slaughtered, Moses' desperate mother placed him in a floating basket in the swamp-thicket of the Nile. His big sister Miriam watched his little bassinette bob among the reeds until Pharaoh's daughter found the infant during her bath. Like a little girl discovering a puppy, she asked her daddy if she could keep him.

> 10 When the child grew older, she took him to Pharaoh's daughter and he became her son. She named him Moses, saying, "I drew him out of the water."
>
> 11 One day, after Moses had grown up . . . (Exodus 2:10-11a)

We know nothing of substance regarding Moses' upbringing. A lot of time passes between the 10th and 11th verses of Exodus 2. And into that time we are left to conjecture what kind of upbringing the adopted grandson of Pharaoh would have known.

At what age did Moses recognize his lineage as a descendant of Israel and the brothers of Joseph? When did he connect his identity to those making bricks for the adobe of Egyptian public works? We do not know. But we can safely presume the foundling of an Egyptian princess fared better than his slave-class kinsmen.

The next few verses offer a great deal of insight into the temperament of the future liberator.

> One day, after Moses had grown up, he went out to where his own people were and watched them at their hard labor. He saw an Egyptian beating a Hebrew, one of his own people. Glancing this way and that and seeing no one, he killed the Egyptian and hid him in the sand.
>
> The next day he went out and saw two Hebrews fighting. He asked the one in the wrong, "Why are you hitting your fellow Hebrew?"
>
> The man said, "Who made you ruler and judge over us? Are you thinking of killing me as you killed the Egyptian?" Then Moses was afraid and thought, "What I did must have become known."
>
> When Pharaoh heard of this, he tried to kill Moses, but Moses fled from Pharaoh and went to live in Midian, where he sat down by a well. (Exodus 10:11-15)

At some point Moses had learned of his Hebrew heritage, and so watching "his own people" at hard labor Moses was clearly enraged. In a fit to singlehandedly set things right, Moses impulsively murdered an Egyptian.

But Moses was uncomfortable in his place as a member of the royal household. Hiding the body, Moses fled when he realized there were witnesses to his deed. Whatever his upbringing, Moses' adoptive status in the household of the Pharaoh granted him no immunity from prosecution and execution for murder.

Moses moved between two worlds; son of a Hebrew, adopted by a princess, raised by the royal family, accused by a kinsman, he was constantly the outsider. Moses was granted neither protection by right of his Pharaoic upbringing, nor inclusion among the enslaved descendants of Israel.

Realizing his isolation, Moses flees to Midian and there the confusion continues. The daughters of Reuel see him as an Egyptian (Exodus 2:19) but have no idea how un-Egyptian Moses happens to be. At this point any hospitality felt encouraging. Marrying Zipporah Moses is welcomed into his father-in-law Jethro's family. Still, Moses harbors the feelings of an outsider. He named his first son Gershom (verse 22), a homonym for the Hebrew word *alien*. Over time

Moses seems to make some peace with his outsider status. His second son's name reflects appreciation for Jethro's kindness. But we only learn of Eliezer when Moses is shipping his wife back to her parents.

> . . . after Moses had sent away his wife Zipporah; his father-in-law Jethro received her and her two sons. One son was named Gershom, for Moses said, "I have become an alien in a foreign land"; and the other was named Eliezer, for he said, "My father's God was my helper; he saved me from the sword of Pharaoh." (Exodus 18:2-4)

The next time we hear about Moses' family dynamics is well after the Exodus. His biological brother and sister, Miriam and Aaron, ridicule Moses for having married a Cushite (Numbers 12).[2] They were jealous because they were not receiving the same honor as their baby brother, so they decided to complain about the skin-color of their sister-in-law. In retribution God afflicts Miriam with leprosy, the most dreaded of all skin conditions. Moses intervenes and she is healed, but the exchange demonstrates how, even after the Exodus, Moses remained disconnected from family and heritage.

All this biographical back-fill illustrates Moses' ongoing struggle with his identity as a leader. Pushed out of the Hebrew nest for his own safety, Moses falls into the arms of a household which never fully accepts him. At the same time he is never quite at home with his Hebrew kinsmen. Moses remains disconnected, partially adopted, and continually rejected. No wonder he spends the remainder of his days wrestling with the ambiguities of his call.

The story of Moses' call is familiar. While taking care of his father-in-law's flock Moses saw the burning bush. There for the first time God self-reveals to Moses as the God of Abraham, Isaac, and Jacob. YHWH[3] has heard the cries of the people and has taken pity for the sake of the patriarchs.

---

[2]   There is much debate regarding when Moses married the Ethiopian (Cushite), but the text offers no additional information as Numbers 12 is the only place she is mentioned.

[3]   When Moses asked God's name in Exodus 3:13, God responds with a word which signifies his name in verse 14. Considered too holy to pronounce, an accurate transliteration of this word has been lost to history. Most English translations signify God's name with the capitalization of the word LORD or the anglicized, JEHOVAH. Attempting to preserve the character of the Hebrew, I have chosen to use the four English characters YHWH for the text representing God's name revealed to Moses.

From the beginning Moses was apprehensive about his own capacity to lead. His first response to YHWH's call was deflection.

> The LORD said, " . . . So now, go. I am sending you to Pharaoh to bring my people the Israelites out of Egypt."

> But Moses said to God, "Who am I that I should go to Pharaoh and bring the Israelites out of Egypt?" (Exodus 3:10 & 11)

> Moses said to God, "Suppose I go to the Israelites and say to them, 'The God of your fathers has sent me to you,' and they ask me, 'What is his name?' Then what shall I tell them?" (Exodus 3:13)

Even after YHWH has told Moses that the Israelites (Exodus 3:18), the Egyptians (Exodus 3:21), and even Pharaoh (Exodus 3:20) would listen to him, Moses asks for more proof.

> Moses answered, "What if they do not believe me or listen to me and say, 'The LORD did not appear to you'?" (Exodus 4:1)

Like free samples left by a salesman, YHWH provides Moses with three miracles he can share with the Israelites and the Egyptians—his staff becoming a snake, his hand becoming leprous, and the waters of the Nile becoming blood. But Moses continues to resist.

> Moses said to the LORD, "O Lord, I have never been eloquent, neither in the past nor since you have spoken to your servant. I am slow of speech and tongue." (Exodus 4:10)

And again,

> Moses said, "O Lord, please send someone else to do it." (Exodus 4:13)

After his first meeting with Pharaoh when the Israelites were told to gather their own straw for brick making,

> Moses returned to the LORD and said, "O Lord, why have you brought trouble upon this people? Is this why you sent me? Ever since I went to Pharaoh to speak in your name, he has brought trouble upon this people, and you have not rescued your people at all." (Exodus 5:22-23)

Then, after the people have complained and YHWH tells Moses to return to Pharaoh,

> Moses said to the LORD, "If the Israelites will not listen to me, why would Pharaoh listen to me, since I speak with faltering lips?" (Exodus 6:12)

And again,

> Moses said to the LORD, "Since I speak with faltering lips, why would Pharaoh listen to me?" (Exodus 6:30)

Even with YHWH's mandate, miracles, and reassurance, Moses continues to argue his inadequacy and unsuitability for national leadership. Moses believes he has no personal charisma and, as such, is unfit for his executive position.

What's more, Moses demonstrates no real affection for the people. (A fact noted by Miriam and Aaron when Moses married outside of the Israelite nation, first Zipporah a Midianite, and then a Cushite.)

In arguments with God, Moses often points out that the Israelites were not *his* people and the Covenant was not with him. Most notably he makes this case with YHWH at Taberah.

> (Moses) asked the LORD, "Why have you brought this trouble on your servant? What have I done to displease you that you put the burden of all these people on me? Did I conceive all these people? Did I give them birth? Why do you tell me to carry them in my arms, as a nurse carries an infant, to the land you promised on oath to their forefathers?" (Numbers 11:11-12)

What drives Moses? By his own admission he lacks commitment to the people of Israel, he has little patience with administration, and feels distant

---

from any connection to the Covenant. Moses is not a man on a mission, he is a reluctant hireling driven by the push of obligation. These were not his people, this was not his skill-set, and the promise wasn't his.

As with his father-in-law's sheep in Midian, Moses is shepherding someone else's flock. He is now tending the offspring of Abraham, Isaac, and Jacob. Moses sees himself as proxy for the patriarchs. YHWH's promise was to them, and Moses merely does the heavy lifting to fulfill a bargain he did not strike.

Moses functions like a beleaguered administrative assistant. Whenever the rank and file becomes cantankerous, Moses reminds YHWH of appointments made long ago with the patriarchs. Keeping the minutes of each meeting, Moses reads the contents of the complaint box to the big boss YHWH, who offers solutions which Moses promptly memos to the tribal rank and file.

When not dealing with communication problems or tracking down supplies, Moses works tirelessly on policy and procedure manuals attempting to cover every contingency regarding religious practice, international relations, social order, and public health. Not once does Moses assert or internalize his right to lead. No wonder he's frequently frustrated and always on the brink of complete burnout.

Twice YHWH offers to destroy the people and give Moses the position of neo-patriarch; in both cases, Moses declines. First, after the mutiny at Camp Sinai in Exodus 32:7-10. God threatens to destroy the people for being "corrupt" (verse 7) and "stiff necked" (verse 9). Moses responds:

> . . ."O LORD," he said, "why should your anger burn against your people, whom you brought out of Egypt with great power and a mighty hand? Why should the Egyptians say, 'It was with evil intent that he brought them out, to kill them in the mountains and to wipe them off the face of the earth'? Turn from your fierce anger; relent and do not bring disaster on your people. Remember your servants Abraham, Isaac and Israel, to whom you swore by your own self: 'I will make your descendants as numerous as the stars in the sky and I will give your descendants all this land I promised them, and it will be their inheritance forever.'" Then the LORD relented and did not bring on his people the disaster he had threatened. (Exodus 32:11-14)

The second time, following the report from the spies in Numbers 14, God complains of being treated with "contempt" (verse 11). Again Moses pleas,

"Then the Egyptians will hear about it! By your power you brought these people up from among them. And they will tell the inhabitants of this land about it. They have already heard that you, O LORD, are with these people and that you, O LORD, have been seen face to face, that your cloud stays over them, and that you go before them in a pillar of cloud by day and a pillar of fire by night. If you put these people to death all at one time, the nations who have heard this report about you will say, 'The LORD was not able to bring these people into the land he promised them on oath; so he slaughtered them in the desert.'

Now may the Lord's strength be displayed, just as you have declared: 'The LORD is slow to anger, abounding in love and forgiving sin and rebellion. Yet he does not leave the guilty unpunished; he punishes the children for the sin of the fathers to the third and fourth generation.' In accordance with your great love, forgive the sin of these people, just as you have pardoned them from the time they left Egypt until now." (Numbers 14:12-19)

In both instances, Moses' defense to spare the nation is not based on any affection for the Israelite people; there is no plea for God to protect the individuals freed from Egyptian slavery. Moses preempts YHWH's destruction by an appeal to YHWH's character as a covenant keeper and YHWH's reputation among the nations. Moses understands his leadership role not through a personal connection to the congregation; instead Moses prevents genocide by appealing to Divine ego.

"What will the Egyptians say about you?" inquires Moses. You wipe out these people and you will be a laughing stock among the nations. Moses' appeal to YHWH is based on Moses' best interest. YHWH's word had better be good, or Moses has nothing left on which to stand.

Unspoken, but in the back of Moses' mind was this concern. If YHWH broke the Covenant with Abraham simply because of the rebellion of Abraham's offspring, how could Moses trust YHWH if Moses' descendants revolt? No, Moses knew he could not supplant the Abrahamic line. Credibility was wrapped in YHWH's Covenant with Abraham, not a new deal with Moses.

Such insecurity breeds caution. And from this cautious perspective Moses cannot articulate vision or possibility. Once vision and possibility are lost, fatigue and impulsive reactivity are quick to take command.

In Kadesh Moses faced personal consequences for his inability to apprehend the full authority of his leadership.

Now there was no water for the community, and the people gathered in opposition to Moses and Aaron. They quarreled with Moses and said, "If only we had died when our brothers fell dead before the LORD! Why did you bring the LORD's community into this desert, that we and our livestock should die here? Why did you bring us up out of Egypt to this terrible place? It has no grain or figs, grapevines or pomegranates. And there is no water to drink!"

Moses and Aaron went from the assembly to the entrance to the Tent of Meeting and fell facedown, and the glory of the LORD appeared to them. The LORD said to Moses, "Take the staff, and you and your brother Aaron gather the assembly together. Speak to that rock before their eyes and it will pour out its water. You will bring water out of the rock for the community so they and their livestock can drink."

So Moses took the staff from the LORD's presence, just as he commanded him. He and Aaron gathered the assembly together in front of the rock and Moses said to them, "Listen, you rebels, must we bring you water out of this rock?" Then Moses raised his arm and struck the rock twice with his staff. Water gushed out, and the community and their livestock drank.

But the LORD said to Moses and Aaron, "Because you did not trust in me enough to honor me as holy in the sight of the Israelites, you will not bring this community into the land I give them." (Numbers 20:2-12)

The error of Moses was not his striking the rock rather than speaking to it. Moses' error was the bravado born of insecure exhaustion. YHWH was the one who would bring water from the rock, not Moses, not Aaron. But Moses announced his personal disgust at needing to produce water, yet again. His inability to articulate the source of his authority rendered him inadequate to be a Promised Land leader.

Moses is remembered as the great law-giver. But his legendary fascination with Levitical and Deuteronomic code seemed to have little impact on his confidence to systematically administer the law through effective management of the people. As a result Moses' tenure was marked by continual exhaustion, periodic brooding, and disgruntled followers who regularly longed for the more "orderly" days of slavery.

Perhaps it was because Moses had grown up with the influence, power, and prestige of Pharaoh's household. Perhaps it was because he was shy and inarticulate, or perhaps it was because he was the only Hebrew male his own age. Regardless of the reason, Moses never quite fit his role as a leader.

On Nebo God took Moses on one last walk for the sole purpose of seeing what he would never touch (Deuteronomy 32:48-52). From the beginning Moses had difficulty owning his leadership identity, and in the end, Moses was denied participation in the final reward of the Exodus.

The implication for religious leaders is significant. *Leaders must first and foremost embrace their identity; they must claim their authority to lead.*

CHAPTER II

The Shape of Authority

At its core, authority is the "right" by which leaders make decisions, *and* (this is the tricky part) their ability to make those decisions "stick".

As Moses' leadership illustrates, when one's "right" to authority is ambiguous, conflict is inevitable. Nowhere is the comprehension of authority more important than in the self-understanding of the leader. Comprehending one's own authority is the beginning of leadership. Or to put it another way, if leaders are not confident regarding the source of their authority, then the organization is headed for trouble.

Ministerial authority requires a shared agreement between the leader and the congregation. Without mutual understanding regarding the right to lead, all the ordination ceremonies, advanced degrees, or winsome charm mean nothing.

Each and every leader must be clear regarding his or her roles and responsibilities within the organization. Disputes may be resolved insofar as the leaders and congregation are in agreement regarding how power is claimed and shared.

Authority for leadership has two dimensions, *external polity*, and *internal orientation*. External polity is the formal expression of a congregation's organization. For most Christian congregations, external polity is expressed through rules for ordination, bylaws for decision making, and policies regarding membership. External polity is the means by which a congregation maintains organizational cohesion.

To be fair, some of Moses' difficulty apprehending his right to authority was due to the complete absence of an established polity for the children of Israel. Prior to the Exodus there was no system by which leadership among the slaves could emerge. (In fact it was fear of an emerging leadership that led Pharaoh to slaughter Moses' infant cohort in Exodus 1:8-22.) Beyond his encounter with the burning bush and a few miraculous presentations, Moses held no formal claim to authority over the children of Israel. He had not been installed, ordained, or certified to the office of liberator. Without a clearly defined external polity, his right to lead was constantly questioned. Likewise, without a formally defined set of qualifications for ministry, pastors and lay leaders hold little authority beyond their own sense of call and their powers of persuasion.

Every Christian denomination asserts that Jesus Christ is the head of the Church that all authority on heaven and earth rests upon him alone (Matthew 28:18-20 and Philippians 2:9-11). But beyond these lofty statements of identity, practical administration requires clarification regarding temporal authority. Who is in charge 'till Kingdom comes?

Polity is the interpretation of the Holy Spirit's work—*pneumatology*. Polity is the means whereby communities seek God's direction. Or to put it another way, polity is how the community identifies the Holy Spirit's "voice".

As Jesus told Nicodemus,

> **"The wind blows wherever it pleases. You hear its sound, but you cannot tell where it comes from or where it is going. So it is with everyone born of the Spirit." (John 3:8)**

The interpretation of where the wind (*pneuma*) is blowing is the work of congregational and denominational polity, and polity identifies the formal source of authority for church leaders.

External definitions of congregational authority divide into three types.[4] Each is reflected in three distinct polities (the ways in which congregations are organized) of the Christian Church. They are:

- Rational-Legal—Reflected in a *Board of Directors* polity
- Inherited-Tradition—Demonstrated through *Episcopal* polity, and
- Charismatic-Personality—Most often seen in *Congregational* polity.

These three forms demonstrate how communities organize around very different understandings of how God's Spirit is discerned through the life of the community.

---

[4]   These three categories I have lifted from *Politics as a Vocation,* by nineteenth-century sociologist Max Weber, in which he describes how power is distributed within a society or organization.

The differences between these polities express corresponding implications for how the Spirit "speaks" (or more to the point is "heard"). They are best understood by seeing how each of these systems of church governance approach specific areas of practical administration: leadership selection, decision making, membership requirements, and congregational coherence. What a denomination says about each of these areas of administration clearly reflects its presuppositions regarding the nature of the Spirit's voice.

If God "speaks" through the thoughtful competencies of precept and understanding, then those demonstrating Rational-Legal proficiency should be in charge. On the other hand, if God "speaks" most clearly through tradition handed down generation to generation, authority must reside with "keepers" of tradition, uncorrupted by the quixotic temptation of new ideas or suave speech. If, however, God speaks to whomever God chooses, then every voice should have opportunity to hold sway, allowing those with the most persuasive gifts to direct the affairs of the community.

Rational-Legal Authority is anchored in impersonal rules legally enacted or contractually established. This authority is *ex officio*, literally *from-the-office*. Rational Legal or *ex officio* authority finds legitimacy from the documents that define the organization. Most modern western organizations, governments, businesses, and religious institutions define power through their constitutions, bylaws, rules of operation, etc. People are promoted, disciplined, rewarded, or removed according to the procedures set forth in these documents. In an *ex officio* system the authority of the individual depends upon the legally defined power of the office.

Rational-Legal Authority is a necessary element in the functioning of a bureaucracy. Bureaucracies afford specifically defined spheres of power and authority to individuals who occupy positions of organizational "space" and thereby become interchangeable over time.

Most religious bodies grant their ministers some form of *ex officio* authority. The denominational handbook, the congregation's constitution, and bylaws specify the rights and responsibilities of their leader(s). State statute (usually followed to ensure a tax exempt housing allowance for clergy) also defines an ordained leader of a religious body and stipulates the role such individuals hold in executing civil functions such as the signing of marriage licenses.

In many denominations, those preparing for ministry spend a great deal of time fulfilling the requirements of *ex officio* authority. Seminary education, ordination exams, psychological interviews, internships, clinical pastoral education, etc. are fulfilled in order to meet documented and codified expectations. Ordained office is held only when one meets these "requirements".

Candidates for ministry identify these standards as "hoops" through which they must jump. Rational-Legal Authority "kicks-in" only after the individual is approved for office. Having fulfilled the requirements of the position, they are presumed to hold authority of the office.

One colleague compared preparation for ministry to "four years of taxiing". The metaphor reflects how the candidate is kept from "taking-off" for a myriad of reasons. But once ordained and installed, the new pastor is expected to fly solo through every possible storm.

Likewise, *ex officio* authority can be lost if the individual violates the statutes of the office. The removal of the individual from office (and the corresponding stripping of authority) requires the individual to be demonstrably in violation of specific standards.

This is why members of most congregations never bother looking at their denomination's organizational documents until they want to remove their pastor. In the middle of conflict previously ignored bylaws and constitutions become extremely important. Copies of the relevant documents are distributed, portions are read aloud at meetings, and sections are highlighted and emailed to the district superintendent, disciplinary committee, or bishop. (As a congregational consultant, I can usually tell how controversial the tenure of a pastor has been by observing the wear and tear on copies of the church's bylaws.)

This is also why church and denominational constitutions become the focal point of controversy in times of social change. The desire is often to limit the power of some category of individuals based on social condition (age, political affiliation, marital status, gender, sexual orientation, etc.). Because Rational-Legal Authority requires codified expression before individuals may be categorically included or excluded from power, changing those provisions becomes the focal point for anxiety and conflict.

The major limit of *ex officio* authority is how the qualifications for office may not correspond with the character necessary for leadership. A candidate for ministry may meet all of the "official" requirements, pass all the necessary exams, attend all the interviews and hearings, yet still be deemed inappropriate for ministry.

On more than one occasion I have counseled ministerial candidates referred to me by their denomination because ordination commission members were uncomfortable approving them for ordained ministry. Without some bureaucratic reason to deny ordination, members of the commission add the requirement of counseling. Occasionally other requirements are added to the standards for ordination with the hope to "weed-out" such candidates in the future. Unfortunately, it is nearly impossible to create constitutional codes which identify individuals who are boring, scatter-brains, or jerks.

Scripture contains a few examples of *ex officio* authority, most notably the portions of the Pastoral Epistles discussing requirements for congregational leaders.

> Here is a trustworthy saying: If anyone sets his heart on being an overseer, he desires a noble task. Now the overseer must be above reproach the husband of but one wife, temperate, self-controlled, respectable, hospitable, able to teach, not given to drunkenness, not violent but gentle, not quarrelsome, not a lover of money. He must manage his own family well and see that his children obey him with proper respect. (If anyone does not know how to manage his own family, how can he take care of God's church?) He must not be a recent convert, or he may become conceited and fall under the same judgment as the devil. He must also have a good reputation with outsiders, so that he will not fall into disgrace and into the devil's trap.
>
> Deacons, likewise, are to be men worthy of respect, sincere, not indulging in much wine, and not pursuing dishonest gain. They must keep hold of the deep truths of the faith with a clear conscience. They must first be tested; and then if there is nothing against them, let them serve as deacons.
>
> In the same way, their wives are to be women worthy of respect, not malicious talkers but temperate and trustworthy in everything.
>
> A deacon must be the husband of but one wife and must manage his children and his household well. Those who have served well gain an excellent standing and great assurance in their faith in Christ Jesus. (I Timothy 3:1-13)

Because these passages convey standards whereby one qualifies for offices of church leadership, these texts are well-thumbed in denominations debating categorical requirements for those seeking ordination. Unfortunately, scripture is lacking a clear, consistent, impersonal, delineated, cross-cultural set of qualifications for leadership.[5]

It is important to note that these instructions for ordination emerged when the first generation of congregational leaders were retiring. Standards became crucial because eyewitnesses to the life of Jesus were dying and the church was entering a difficult phase, the transfer of power to the second generation.

Organizations living beyond their founders often experience a crisis of authority because the first generation's "right to power" usually flows from a specific experience which connected them to the second type of authority, Inherited-Tradition.

Inherited-Tradition Authority, most clearly seen in monarchies, is based on belief in the sanctity of inheritance (what the German sociologist Max Weber delightfully called the power of the "eternal yesterday").

Inherited-Tradition is not codified by impersonal standards. Holders of inherited tradition often make up their own rules. Inherited-Tradition falls to particular persons who either receive it as a family right or are invested with it by the authority of the retiring generation.

This is the authority of ancient priests, kings, and executives in family-owned businesses. The right to rule is passed-down from one individual to another independent of objective measures. For example, when Moses anointed Aaron and Aaron's sons to serve as the first priests of the Tabernacle, all Levites after them are granted priestly authority by birth, not by competence or personality.

> "Bring Aaron and his sons to the entrance to the Tent of Meeting and wash them with water. Then dress Aaron in the sacred garments, anoint him and consecrate him so he may serve me as priest. Bring his sons and dress them in tunics. Anoint them just as you anointed their father, so they may serve me as priests. Their anointing will be to a priesthood that will continue for all generations to come." Moses did everything just as the LORD commanded him. (Exodus 40:12-16)

---

[5] For example, the Larger Westminster Catechism identifies the singing of lascivious songs and attendance of stage plays as clear violations of the seventh commandment (7.249.Q139). In addition, few modern denominations follow the scriptural admonition for women to never braid their hair (I Timothy 2:9 and I Peter 3:3).

Note the only reason Moses' nephews are anointed as priests is because they happen to be sons of Aaron. Likewise, Aaron's own ordination was dependent upon his blood relationship to Moses.

Inherited-Tradition in many congregations definitely flows toward some individuals based on their historic, economic, or social position (e.g. charter members, long-time Sunday school superintendent, influential executive, etc.). Sadly, Inherited-Tradition may be dissociated from competence. Decisions are made which affect the whole community, but those decisions "stick" because the people who made them hold Inherited-Tradition Authority.

Combatants in established churches usually find battle-lines drawn between *traditional* and *ex officio* leaders, as duly elected-officers square-off against unelected bearers of tradition. Every new pastor has come home after a committee or council meeting delighted over the new course chartered with a spirit of unity and enthusiasm, only to have every decision evaporate a few days later when examined under the withering disapproval of Inherited-Tradition Authority.

In fact, denominations struggling with proposed changes to ordination qualifications most frequently appeal to *Traditional Authority* in rejecting standards of *Rational Authority*. Delegates may have every *rational* reason to change ordination standards in order to include groups of individuals previously categorically denied ordination, but appeals to *tradition* prevent such changes. For example, denominations resisting the ordination of qualified women do so by appeal to tradition, not reason.

In every organization some individuals are afforded disproportional decision-making power, even in areas where they have no expertise or authority. They are "in-charge" simply because of their historic traditional ties to the organization.

When facing the power of tradition, leaders frequently make one of two fundamental errors. First, leadership tends to underestimate the power of Inherited-Tradition.

A friend of mine ministering in a small town knows that every decision made by his church board is reviewed for ratification or rejection the following morning when the "town fathers" gather for coffee at the café on Main Street. This informal gathering has representation from every major congregation in town, most of whom are direct descendants of their congregation's charter members. Without minutes, bylaws, constitution, or elected officers, they collectively hold the final decision-making power for every main-line congregation in town.

While my friend would have every constitutional right to override their recommendations, he knows they, in turn would use every constitutional means to remove him from his pastorate. In his town *ex officio* authority is subservient to Traditional Authority. When challenged, tradition wins.

But Inherited-Tradition does not only serve as a roadblock to a "more effective" Rational-Legal functioning. Inherited-Tradition can be extremely useful in settling petty disputes.

One congregation, in which I served as pastor, would refer every year to a Christmas card photo of the sanctuary printed in the 1950's for instructions on how they were to decorate the chancel for Advent. Any attempt to deviate from the tradition captured in the photograph met with swift opposition. Tradition always trumped innovation. I found this comforting as there was expedience in not having to re-invent the chancel decorations every year.

Likewise, a number of years ago I attended a board meeting of a large urban congregation. The beloved long-tenured pastor had retired and the new minister was proposing changes to the long-established order of worship. This new pastor wanted to have the elders (his Rational-Legal body) "on-board" with the proposed changes and so he called a special meeting to discuss the changes.

The meeting began with a lengthy presentation by a professor of liturgy from a denominational seminary. His presentation traced the theological history of the current and proposed orders of worship. In a measured and balanced fashion the merits of order were explained and theological priorities were discussed. As I looked around the room I noticed several elders nodding off, others doodled on their notepads; one elder studied hairline cracks in the ceiling.

Following the professorial dissertation, the senior pastor presented his case for the new sequence of worship. To the same distracted attention of his elders, he passionately explained how the new order was more appropriate to the modern age, to his theological understanding, and to the needs of the community. There was then time on the agenda for questions. There were few.

The pastor, taking seriously the *ex officio* role of his elders, wanted each to "weigh in" on the decision, so prior to the vote each and every board member was invited to share his or her thoughts. After a long silence, one of the elders, a retired female corporate executive, said, "As far as I'm concerned, you're the pastor, it's your worship service. Do what you want!"

A motion was made to adopt the new order of worship, seconded, and passed by an overwhelming majority. The transition to a new Sunday liturgy occurred unremarkably; much to the delight of the new pastor who believed his educational preparation and adherence to a Rational-Legal process were the reasons for his success.

Reflecting with a colleague a few days later, I realized that the pastor had miscalculated the location of his authority in that institution. Mustering the forces of a Rational-Legal appeal he was ready to take on the traditionalists by rigidly adhering to a constitutional process. The elders were the duly qualified deliberative body and their recently installed pastor wanted to assure them that their *ex officio* authority would be respected.

What the pastor failed to understand was how Inherited-Tradition was what held sway in that congregation. Now that he sat in the seat of Inherited-Tradition, wielding the Traditional Authority was not the right of the elders, it was his. "It's your worship service. Do what you want!"

The second mistake leaders often make when encountering conflict between *ex officio* and Traditional Authority is to assume the organization can cohere without ultimately taking a stand.

In the end, one form of authority *will* hold sway, and inconsistently moving back and forth between the two can shake an organization apart. As a consultant I am amazed how frequently leaders claim their authority by organizational charts in one context, and tradition in another.

Organizational leaders, like leaders of whole societies, must be clear regarding the underlying pillars of power. If a constitution is to be suspended in defense of tradition, or bylaws disregarded in the name of expedience, then the members of the organization should be ready to play fully by the traditionalist's rules. Like my pastor friend who could be vetoed by the coffee circle, Inherited-Tradition Authority does not wield its influence occasionally.

If, on the other hand, traditionalists don't get their way because the officers have rationally chosen a different course (based on bylaws or rules), the leadership should not participate in sabotage that undercuts the authority of the office holders.

Too often leaders appeal to *ex officio* authority in one context and Traditional Authority in another, selecting their appeal based on the expedience of what will allow them to "win" in the short run, not based on how the organization will best cohere for coming generations.

Leaders, however, get into the greatest trouble wielding the third type of authority.

Charismatic-Personality Authority rests on the appeal of leaders who legitimate allegiance because of their extraordinary virtuosity—heroism, good looks, vitality, wit, or character.

The term *Charismatic-Personality* should not be confused with the religious experience of the *charismatic movement*, whereby individuals validate the outpouring of the Holy Spirit by ecstatic utterances of tongues and prophecy. Application of a charismatic experience can also confirm Rational-Legal or Traditional Authority (see the discussion of Numbers

11:26-30 in Chapter III). A charismatic style of worship can occur in any organizational setting.

Charismatic-Personality Authority carries the connotation that the individual's right to lead is the consequence of personal gifts, the legitimacy of which is based upon the response of the followers. Charismatic leaders may be constitutionally elected or traditionally anointed, but once in power they use their "charms" to persuade others to surrender a disproportionate level of authority to them. Power for them is legitimated in the relationship between leader and follower. It is the power of the televangelist, the cult-leader, the magnetic personality that spellbinds the masses to obedience.

What makes Charismatic-Personality Authority so dangerous is its self-referencing quality. The leader derives his/her position not from what the followers believe regarding mission, but their willingness to allow the charismatic leader to define the mission unilaterally. Absent an external reference, the possibility of checks and balances are dangerously limited when Charismatic Authority is invoked. This is why Scripture provides the following warning against charisma.

> If a prophet, or one who foretells by dreams, appears among you and announces to you a miraculous sign or wonder, and if the sign or wonder of which he has spoken takes place, and he says, "Let us follow other gods" (gods you have not known) "and let us worship them," you must not listen to the words of that prophet or dreamer. The LORD your God is testing you to find out whether you love him with all your heart and with all your soul. (Deuteronomy 13:1-3)

Try as we might, we are prone to persuasion by the charismatic leader. I've met beaming church members who, in addition to listing degrees and skills of their beloved pastor, cannot help but add, "And he's so good looking," or "She's just as cute as a button!"

Because Charismatic Authority is so persuasive, every minister has attempted to affect the right smile, gestures, carriage, or wardrobe, in an attempt to add charisma to their arsenal of qualifications. "Looking the part" is reasonable, unless it becomes the only reason to have the part.

Charismatic Authority is not always "friendly" charm. Equally powerful is a charisma of fear wielded by individuals who exercise control and influence well beyond the power of their competence or office, simply because they are too frightening to challenge.

The fundamental problem with Charismatic Authority is the abdication of sound judgment on the part of the congregation. By fear or flattery, charismatic leaders remove from their followers all right to doubt. Trust is exclusively in the leader, not to a connection with tradition, ideals, or due process.

Opposition and the Shape of Authority

Individuals within an organization may find multiple dimensions for their own authority, occasionally appealing to all three, competence, charm, and birthright. But organizationally, the structure and tradition of the institution will indicate an unambiguous preference.

Opposition to any form of authority always arises from one of the other two positions. Charismatic-Personality Authority will be challenged by Rational-Legal or Traditional arguments. Inherited-Tradition is often overthrown by Rational-Legal tests of competence or dismissed as too fuddy-duddy, and duly appointed *ex officio* officers are often overthrown by more charming up-and-comers or the keepers of the old-guard.

Once leadership recognizes the basic shape of their tradition's authority, be it Rational-Legal, Traditional, or Charismatic, they must be prepared for the arguments put forth by the adherents to the neglected forms. Fundamental to understanding the opposition is recognizing how their differing standards for authority create the basis for their distrust.

Polity and Pneumatology

As mentioned above, each of the three sources of authority are reflected in denominational polities. Polity for a denomination is the means whereby authority is identified and power is maintained.

Presbyterian or Representative Polity

In a Presbyterian or representative polity God is perceived to speak to all individuals but some individuals are qualified, and thereby "recognized" for positions of leadership. Recognition of qualification is determined through examination. There is a strong emphasis on the participatory rights and spiritual responsibilities of every individual, but authority is reserved for groups of individuals expressing their will through councils and committees. Since the Spirit is believed to communicate through the system, attention is given to the process rather than lines of authority or spiritual insight.

Representative Polity Leadership: Leaders are selected from and granted authority by the collective will of the membership. Personal characteristics are evaluated based upon the individual's capacity to fulfill the duties of the office and authority may be rescinded through the will of the community expressed through a defined orderly process. The authority is maintained by the office but does not "sanctify" the office-holder. This means individual leaders must maintain personal, spiritual, and behavioral decorum. Because a leader's abilities may change over time, individuals ordinarily serve for pre-determined terms of office. Expectations of human condition (e.g. gender, orientation, social participation, and discipline) tend to reflect the social expressions of the community rather than the mandates of tradition.

Representative Polity Decision Making: The authority to make decisions tends to rest in commissions, councils, and committees, with the general membership selecting the individuals serving on these decision making bodies. These groups uphold the processes whereby dissent is heard and weighed as part of their deliberation.

Representative Polity Membership: Standards for membership tend to lessen the regard for personal or social condition and focus more on participation and mutual support. Those who hold certain offices have the responsibility to adjudicate levels of participation within the group.

Representative Polity Cohesiveness: Presbyterian or representative/elder groups tend to be coherent insofar as they reflect the shared values of the congregational community. Schism tends to occur around issues of authority when process has been circumvented or when individuals or groups step beyond the scope of their constitutionally defined authority.

Hierarchical or Episcopal Polity

Hierarchical polity perceives God speaking to and through specific offices set forth by ancient tradition (e.g. Papacy, Bishopric, or Vicar). There is a strong emphasis in hierarchical systems on the rites and responsibilities of various offices and their proportional authority relative to other offices. Since the Spirit communicates from the "top down", each successive level of administration is absolutely accountable to the level above it.

Hierarchical Polity Leadership: Standards for leadership in hierarchical systems begin with evaluations of human condition (e.g. gender, sexual practice/orientation, social context, or birthright). Leadership is self-appointing and authority is held for life because the office is perceived to "sanctify" the individual. Each ascending level of authority holds near absolute power over lower offices, demanding unwavering obedience because the higher positions are understood to be closer to The Divine.

Hierarchical Polity Decision Making: Decision making, like authority is "top down". Authority resides in the office and not the individual and so each leader makes decisions in light of the historic precedent of tradition, usually defended as an unbroken line of succession. Change is often distrusted and avoided, and there is virtually no authority granted for dissent by members.

Hierarchical Polity Membership: Because congregation members function at the lowest level of the system, their core responsibility is to comply with expectations given by those who are in authority over them. Identification with the group is determined by the hierarchy and is contingent upon the hierarchy's confirmation. Standards for membership tend to be ritualized and independent of the condition or character of the members. Member participation in administration is limited since access to what the officials determine to be "holy" is reserved for those who are the keepers of the tradition. Excommunication is the ultimate punishment for non-compliance. Full participation in membership is limited to those supporting and enacting the mission and values are set by those in authority.

Hierarchical Polity Cohesiveness: Because hierarchical systems recognize the authority of office they tend to be very cohesive. Schisms tend to develop only over the rites of office and the consistency of innovations in relationship to historic precedence.

Charismatic or Congregational Polity

Congregational polity perceives God speaking most clearly and directly to the hearts of individuals. There is a strong emphasis on the spirituality of the individual, with a focus on the cultivation of the soul through private spiritual discipline. The organization exists to cultivate these private disciplines, usually the reading of scripture and prayer to "sanctify" personal behavior.

Charismatic Polity Leadership: Congregational polity downplays the authority of clergy, and some traditions dismiss the role of ordination altogether. Leaders are usually elected, and systems for removal from leadership tend to appear quite simple. If an individual in leadership demonstrates "inappropriate" spiritual or personal characteristics they are removed from positions of authority insofar as a majority of the membership decides.

Charismatic Polity Decision Making: Because God "speaks" through individuals, decision making involves broad participation. Full access to authority is offered to each and every individual perceived to be "in-tune" with the Spirit.

Charismatic Polity Membership: Standards for membership in a congregational system are usually high. Public expressions of personal salvation are often required and participation in study groups, prayer meetings, and worship are carefully scrutinized. Individuals exhibiting unapproved behavior may be prohibited from full participation in membership because those activities are perceived to limit one's capacity to "hear" the Spirit. These conditions may include gender, marital status, sexual orientation, and/or contact with "profane" activities (e.g. smoking, drinking, dancing, going to movies, etc.).

Charismatic Polity Cohesiveness: Congregational systems tend to be internally cohesive with clear expectations regarding consistency of participation and behavior. But because identification with the group requires consistency, schism is common. New groups split and form around new interpretations or standards. Those disagreeing with newly revealed insights are dismissed as "unspiritual" and continued association becomes impossible.

External Authority in the Time of Moses and Joshua

Moses' authority was of the traditional type. Called to be shoeless at the burning bush, Moses' authority rested neither on constitutional compliance nor personal charisma, but upon God's imposition of authority. God simply stated the "eternal yesterday" of Abraham, Isaac, and Jacob.

> 'Go, I am sending you to Pharaoh to bring my people, the Israelites, out of Egypt.' (Exodus 3:10)

Moses attempted to deflect God's call, first by appealing to a Rational-Legal assessment. Moses asked,

> 'Who am I, that I should go to Pharaoh and bring the Israelites out of Egypt?' (Exodus 3:11)

Moses then tried to step aside by discounting his charismatic capacity.

> Moses said to the LORD, 'O Lord, I have never been eloquent, neither in the past nor since you have spoken to your servant. I am slow of speech and tongue.' (Exodus 4:10)

Neither of these attempts worked.

Inherited-Tradition Authority was also the type held by Egyptian Pharaohs. The difference between Pharaoh's and Moses' authority was not type, but deity. The right to lead was Inherited-Tradition, it was bound in divine mandate; authority for the Exodus was between warring gods. Through the plagues, the God of the Israelites demonstrated greater power than the gods of the Pharaoh. At the crossing of the sea, the Egyptian army was defeated when Moses used his God granted authority to flood horse and rider.

No wonder the people perceived their disputes best settled by Moses. Who else held such power? While there were other wise ones in the camp, only Moses had been called by the burning bush, only Moses could anoint Aaron, only Moses could call down locusts and the angel of death, only Moses could split the waters. Why go anywhere else?

When the people were complaining about the lack of meat, they cried out to Moses hoping to change their plight. Moses complained to God in an attempt to reject his calling, but his calling was neither his choice nor avoidable. Moses was endowed with all the power of the Divine. Unless God transferred some of that authority to another, Moses alone was called to lead the people.

Even Joshua's wisdom and obvious charisma could not override the power of Moses' authority. When Moses accepted the intelligence report of the ten other spies in Numbers 13, Joshua, together with Caleb, was ignored. In the same way, Joshua's wisdom was dismissed when he warned Moses against the charisma of two who prophesied in Numbers 11. Even though Joshua was the designated heir apparent (Deuteronomy 31), Moses held all the Inherited-Tradition Authority until the day of his death.

Crucial for each and every leader is an understanding of his or her congregation's external polity and underlying pneumatology. Authority without shared context is disruptive, and in the end will be withdrawn. A Catholic priest operating under Episcopal polity may have many parishioners attracted to his charisma, but when he speaks beyond the scope of tradition, those in authority will discipline and even remove him, regardless of the impact on attendance. On the other hand, a charismatic preacher serving under a congregational polity may break with tradition without any problem, as long as the pews and the offering plates remain full.

Miscalculating the source of authority can result in the miscalculation of one's entire ministry. I suggest aspiring ministers examine their ordaining denomination to discern the "fit" of their pneumatology and structure. A misfit of these elements can destroy both pastors and congregations. Pastoral ministry is hard enough without fundamental conflicts over roles and responsibilities in decision making.

In the end, the fullness of authority is not simply the power to get others to do your bidding; it includes the capacity to keep one's self[6] empowered, even when the group goes limp.

---

[6]   While the term may appropriately be "oneself," I find it helpful to think of the *self* as one of the many constituencies for which the leader is responsible, perhaps the most important constituent.

CHAPTER III

Oriented Leadership

W hile all ministries occur within a polity-framework, true leadership does not begin with a mastery over information, inclusion in a traditional group, or the laudatory affirmation of adoring crowds. The most important basis for ministerial authority begins with an orientation of one's self in relationship to God's call. But claiming authority rooted in one's "call" is a bit like seeking respect or credibility; the more you insist you possess it, the less you probably have it.

Most grounds for authority feel insufficient because of their dependent quality. Reliance on certification, birthright, or charm fades quickly when others no longer concur with these standards.

Each of the three forms of authority mentioned in the previous chapter reference societal structures and group response. Inherited-Tradition Authority rests on a social agreement regarding the past, having authorization passed down by former holders of authority, and grants one a right to power. Rational-Legal Authority rests on a shared understanding of what constitutes competence. And Charismatic Authority is as fleeting as good looks and as vulnerable as a naked emperor.

As the only Israelite to accompany Moses up Mt. Sinai (Exodus 24:13) to be blessed directly as Moses' successor (Deuteronomy 34:9), and as one capable to persuade men into battle (Exodus 17:9), Joshua could lay valid claim to all three forms of authority. But Joshua never referred to external validation for this leadership. He had something more which gave him both inner strength and outer creditability. Joshua had Oriented Leadership.

Oriented Leadership—More Than "Vision"

When meeting with pastors and church officers, I often find them quick to blame the struggles of their congregations on the lack of vision. "I would love for that to happen at my church, but *my* church lacks that kind of vision." (I have even heard these words come out of my own mouth.) The fact is, that's rubbish.

Vision is something congregations claim they desire but seldom *choose* to have. I say choose, because the vision does not come from bright lights on the road or angelic intervention. Vision, like the simple act of orientation, begins by looking around.

Vision requires orientation. Without a connection to the present reality, vision is nothing more than a misguided exuberance or a sign of mental illness.

The congregation in which I grew up was located in the downtown area of a medium-sized city. At a time when suburban sprawl and the heyday of covered malls had moved all commerce to the outskirts of town, the congregation of approximately 800 was comprised of Sunday morning commuters. The building, efficiently constructed in the 1920's, was of no architectural significance and the growing number of alcoholics and prostitutes who gathered at the doors following any evening meeting, made the white middle-class membership uncomfortable.

When I was about ten years old, the congregation's board put together a taskforce to identify property for purchase and relocation. Once they identified a suitable location, the bylaws required congregational approval to secure a mortgage, purchase the land, and retain an architect.

At the congregational meeting one young member stepped forward with a map of the city. He had identified that the best location for the congregation was not the suburban parcel chosen by the taskforce, but in the inner-city—smack dab in the middle of an impoverished African-American neighborhood with a growing indigent population.

His presentation was full of prophetic rhetoric calling the Church to care for the least of God's children. The congregation, relatively affluent and uniformly white, was mostly amused by his youthful vigor. This passionate child of the 1960's held something of a disoriented vision. He believed he could instantaneously change the values of a congregation clearly dedicated to moving up and moving out.

I remember thinking he was somehow right. The congregation was abandoning those whom Christ called us to serve. At the same time, however, I sensed he was strangely out of touch.

In the silence that followed his presentation, he felt dejected. He announced that the congregation lacked true Christian vision, and his counter motion to construct the congregation's new building in the heart of the ghetto died for lack of a second. Even great and faithful ideas die when they are detached from the present reality.

This is equally true for congregations that remain in place not out of commitment but out of inertia. "We need vision!" The people cry as they scamper for institutional survival. Vision, however, is not something one can grab as a last resort. If things are falling apart and the end is near, the sudden injection of vision will not turn the tide of inevitable destruction.

This was the lamentable position of the prophet Jeremiah who had clear vision of what was to come, and that vision included clear recognition of the people's inability to turn things around. Last-ditch clarity is nothing more than an accurate description of the ditch.

Orientation to the Present Reality

Vision must be oriented in the present reality. Audits, assessments, and sometimes just listening, are orientation's tools.

Congregations often take orienting steps when there is a change in pastoral leadership. Membership-rolls are reviewed, audits occur, staffing needs are assessed, and leadership is interviewed. Often congregations will indulge a new pastor with these steps, sensing that he/she needs to gather data in order to take charge.

In reality, these simple steps of orientation are necessary for the whole organization to re-orient, not in light of new leadership, but in light of the present reality.

The new pastor of one congregation was extremely frustrated because he believed worship attendance to be quite low given the total membership of the congregation. They averaged 80-90 in worship, but the membership was recorded as nearly 400. Thumbing through the church directory he realized the congregation's mailing list contained less than 200 names. After reviewing the church rolls he discovered the real membership was closer to 140.

Suddenly, he felt much better about the worship attendance which jumped from 22% of active members to nearly 65% in less than one week of careful orientation! This also changed his perception of the visitation load, as he was no longer feeling the pressure of 250 unmet members.

How did this congregation become so disoriented? A previous pastor refused to change the "count" of members as participation declined, claiming the people would feel better about themselves if they believed they were a mid-sized congregation rather than a small one. Such "cooking-the-books" did little to change the reality of their size, and only confused the leadership when the new pastor asked for a list of the names for all 400 "members". Such a list did not exist.

Orientation also includes financial records, historic records, and demographic analysis. The point in reviewing these documents is to be oriented, to know exactly where the people are standing before the leaders chart the course for movement.

A key step towards orientation is an honest evaluation of a congregation's capacity. For vision to effect change there must be the capacity to change.

To this end, immediately after crossing the Jordan, Joshua inspects and enrolls the Israelite nation. The rite of circumcision had not been performed for the past four decades. Performing this rite on every male (something that can be done only once) allowed Joshua a complete census of the male population. In the process of circumcision and the necessary period of healing, Joshua learned the approximate age, relative health, and the character of his untested army, tribe by tribe, clan by clan, man by man.

> Now when all the Amorite kings west of the Jordan and all the Canaanite kings along the coast heard how the LORD had dried up the Jordan before the Israelites until we had crossed over, their hearts melted and they no longer had the courage to face the Israelites.
>
> At that time the LORD said to Joshua, "Make flint knives and circumcise the Israelites again." So Joshua made flint knives and circumcised the Israelites at Gibeath Haaraloth.
>
> Now this is why he did so: All those who came out of Egypt—all the men of military age—died in the desert on the way after leaving Egypt. All the people that came out had been circumcised, but all the people born in the desert during the journey from Egypt had not. The Israelites had moved about in the desert forty years until all the men who were of military age when they left Egypt had died, since they had not obeyed the LORD. For the LORD had sworn to them that they would not see the land that he had solemnly promised their fathers to give us, a land flowing with milk and honey. So he raised up their sons in their place, and these were the ones Joshua circumcised. They were still

uncircumcised because they had not been circumcised on the way. And after the whole nation had been circumcised, they remained where they were in camp until they were healed.

Then the LORD said to Joshua, "Today I have rolled away the reproach of Egypt from you." So the place has been called Gilgal *(meaning rolling)* to this day. (Joshua 5:1-9)

While this kind of intimate analysis of congregational leadership would be unadvisable in a modern context, knowing the character, age, and health of one's members is a vital first step in orienting them towards movement.

Orientation to History

Following the rite of circumcision Joshua undertakes a second step towards orientation; he ensured the celebration of the Passover.

On the evening of the fourteenth day of the month, while camped at Gilgal on the plains of Jericho, the Israelites celebrated the Passover. (Joshua 5:10)

This was the first celebration in the Land of Promise. But unlike circumcision, Passover seems to have been celebrated annually throughout the forty years of wandering (see Numbers 9).

This first Promised Land celebration oriented the people's present reality to their historic identity. The Passover had been celebrated by their parents and grandparents while on Egyptian soil. It was their first defining act as a people the night before the Exodus, and it became an annual reminder of their identity as a liberated nation.

Oriented Leadership connects the people's present to their past. True orientation remembers, allowing vision to rejuvenate identity. Vision without historic continuity becomes detached and risks being treated as a transplant.

Many pastors with flourishing ministries have written books and how-to manuals for energizing lethargic congregations. The greatest problem with transplantation, however, is the likelihood of rejection. The host body experiences the new program or dynamic idea as an intruder and musters every resistant cell to destroy it.

This does not mean that programs and ideas from other congregations are not transferable. We can learn a great deal from others who have done things well, but there is a fundamental difference between changing hearts and changing the "programmatic" channel.

Innovation that empties the pews of current members and replaces them with different members who are "on-board" with the new program, transforms no one. New ideas, regardless of how creative or coherent they may be, cannot substitute for the healthy functioning of a congregation rooted in the historic identity of their community. If a congregation, and in particular the leadership, are unable to connect past identity to future possibility, they may change the personnel, but will not change hearts.

For every flourishing congregation that has adopted new styles of worship, innovative programs for growth, or creative ideas for outreach, there are an equal number of congregations torn apart by the implementation of the same changes. What most frequently drives members away is how the changes trivialize the congregation's history.

The words "we've never done it that way before" have become a cliché pastors use to describe opposition to change. This phrase together with the phrase "we tried that once, it didn't work" have been identified as the seven last words of the church.

Effective transformation requires continuity. The most effective changes are those which tap the long-standing character of the organization so deeply that the new is not received as a threat, but merely a fuller expression of "what we have been doing all along".

Neither Joshua nor Moses had the luxury of welcoming new members into the covenant community. The alienation of the "old guard" in order to attract promising visitors was not an option. Joshua and Moses were called to lead the descendents of Israel. There were no suggestions that unhappy Hebrews find somewhere else to worship, no welcoming "door-hangers" were placed on the tent-flaps of the Amorites, and no outreach teams visited the Canaanites to replace despondent the Israelites. The children Moses led out of Egypt were the adults Joshua brought into the Promised Land.

As a consultant I have read countless congregational histories. In most cases, the initial years of a congregation's life are full of excitement, growth and possibility. Building projects, program expansion, mission trips, leadership development, and community outreach mark the opening pages of these documents, usually compiled to honor some milestone anniversary in their corporate life.

These documents recalling history, however, are shaped by present reality. Congregations that continue to move, grow, and adapt, spend little space recounting the glories of their past. Their recorded histories identify threads of continuity tying past success to present strength. Innovations for the future are not seen as transplanted ideas, but as reasonable extensions of their founding DNA.

—

Histories of declining congregations usually highlight the discontinuity between their current struggles and their "glory-days". Even congregations with modest beginnings, now facing decline, hearken back to their most aggressively successful points of history as if to magnify the insufficiency of their present reality.

In response to congregational deterioration, *life-cycle theory* has been applied as a descriptive metaphor to account for a congregation's decline. *Life-cycle theory* postulates that institutions mirror human development. A congregation is born, grows, lives, flourishes, deteriorates, remembers, and dies. While this may provide justification for judicatories to "pull-the-plug" of financial life-support for floundering congregations, it does little to explain why some congregations have an unending mid-life renaissance.

Regardless of their age or size, strong congregations look toward the future with confidence because their historic orientation consistently points to the future.

Joshua knew there would be many battles ahead for his young army. He also knew the strength and endurance for these battles would arise from a deep understanding of the people's history expressed in the ritual of the Passover, a liturgy which anchored future hope in past identity.

Orientation to the Eternal

Joshua's deepest orientation, however, occurred when he encountered another warrior-commander in the 5th chapter of the book of Joshua. This encounter occurred on the eve of his first Jericho parade-drill.

> Now when Joshua was near Jericho, he looked up and saw a man standing in front of him with a drawn sword in his hand. Joshua went up to him and asked, "Are you for us or for our enemies?"
>
> "Neither," he replied, "but as commander of the army of the LORD I have now come." Then Joshua fell facedown to the ground in reverence, and asked him,
>
> "What message does my Lord have for his servant?"
>
> The commander of the LORD's army replied, "Take off your sandals, for the place where you are standing is holy." And Joshua did so. (Joshua 5:10-15)

Following the celebration of the first Passover meal grown in promised soil, Joshua takes a nervous walk. He knew the next seven days would make or break his command. Either the Israelites would be shaped into an organized fighting force during the coming week of intensive discipline, or they would become scattered about like un-penned sheep. The daily silent march around Jericho would demonstrate their mettle as an army and his capacity as a commander.

There on the outskirts of the shuttered fortress Jericho, Joshua needed time to think. Since he was a young man (Numbers 11:28) Joshua had been waiting for this moment to lead. Gone was the impediment of Moses' insecurity. Gone was the first generation whose slave-mentality limited their capacity for action. Gone was the malleable Aaron who bowed to the whims of the crowd. Joshua was in charge now and the next seven days would confirm or deny the right of his commission.

Until that time Joshua had lived with a single purpose, to conquer and possess the land promised centuries before to Abraham. Now Joshua walked only a few hundred yards and a few short hours from the beginning of that conquest.

Warrior that he was, it is no wonder he shouted the watchman's call when he encountered the stranger with a drawn sword. "Friend or Foe?" echoed the command-voice of the Israelites. Was this to be his first confirmed kill west of Jordan?

The response of the stranger reoriented Joshua toward an authority beyond anything he had ever imagined, even greater than the success or failure of this military conquest.

"Neither!"

Shouted back the stranger,

"But as commander of the army of the LORD I have now come." (verse 14)

Many Christian commentators, eager to place the eternal Christ in the pages of the Hebrew Scriptures, have identified the stranger as none other than Jesus himself, the Eternal Messiah, appearing to his namesake Joshua. Regardless of whether or not this is a manifestation of the living trinity, it is far more significant that this transcendent commander refuses to pick sides.

Therein lies the most orienting and disorienting question of human authority, "What if the commander of all eternity doesn't choose our side—what if we fail?"

Here rests the final analysis of all human enterprise. Even in the most consecrated activities of a faithful congregation, God is not impressed.

Even after we've heard the sermons, read the manuals, implemented the programs, defended the budgets, led the stewardship campaigns, built the buildings, filled the stadiums, distributed the literature, built the hospitals, formed the seminaries, transformed the culture, if any of it was performed to persuade the Almighty's support, its orientation is sadly flawed.

I have sat through congregational meetings where the purchase of new Hymnals has been defended as God's only choice for a congregation. I have listened to pastors argue that the addition of a staff-member to the church payroll would mean more souls in heaven. I have seen congregations abandon struggling neighborhoods because they believed the suburbs were the modern Promised Land. And in most cases I've cringed, because in these human disputes the commander of the army of the LORD is unambiguously and profoundly non-aligned.

If God was going to fight on the side of any earthly commander, certainly Joshua would have been the man. Here stood the general who would make good the Abrahamic Covenant. This was the one anointed by Moses the law-giver, tempered by the heat of the desert, competent to shape a rag-tag people into a powerful fighting force. But there on the outskirts of Jericho, God remains uncommitted.

What confirms Joshua's orientation is his response. Immediately, without explanation or negotiation, Joshua drops to his knees subjugating his purpose to Divine will. In this submissive posture before The Eternal, Joshua is firmly oriented. *Only in this same submission will our best plans find their orientation.*

On the eve of Jericho, Joshua oriented his goals independent of the success or failure of the conquest. He was serving the Great Commander and the allegiance of the Israelites became something they would need to determine for themselves. If they chose wholehearted dedication to the conquest ahead, Joshua would continue; if they chose another path, Joshua's direction would remain unchanged.

In ministry we command, we organize, we discipline, and we lead. But to be faithful we must do so from this subservient position. Our plans, no matter how righteous, are but dependent projections of our best guess. At any given moment disaster can unravel temporal plots.

To allow the success of our mission to become bigger than our commitment to truth, is to set ourselves on a perilous path. Finding perhaps the success of our goals, we lose our orientation towards what is right.[7]

Unlike Moses at the burning bush, Joshua enters no shoeless negotiation, no stammering doubt, no suggestion of alternatives; Joshua offers only the oriented position of proportion. Joshua's posture oriented his heart. From this subservient position he could see the defeat of Jericho and subsequent victories as the consequence only of God's sovereign option. Perhaps this was *not* going to be the time in which the Covenant would be fulfilled, perhaps Joshua was not going to witness the final settlement, perhaps additional defeat was all that lay ahead. Joshua could not know, and would not hazard a guess. He was kneeling before The Eternal, knowing his best expression of human leadership was to submit his command obediently to the power of eternity.

Oriented Leadership knows its proportion. *Greatness is best expressed in its willingness to bow before that which is greater still.*

---

[7]   I am reminded of two statements attributed to Abraham Lincoln. The first, when Lincoln was assured by an aide that God was on the side of the Union, Lincoln responded, "Sir, my concern is not whether God is on our side; my greatest concern is to be on God's side, for God is always right." Closely paralleling this thought is another attributed quote "I am not bound to win, but I am bound to be true. I am not bound to succeed, but I am bound to live by the light that I have. I must stand with anybody that stands right, and stand with him while he is right, and part with him when he goes wrong." Oriented Authority sees beyond the relative success or failure of accomplishment to the greater purpose of truth.

CHAPTER IV

Leadership Through Change

Change management is a misnomer. Management implies the leader merely guides the energies of an evolving organization into the right channel. Nothing could be farther from the truth!

Those seeking change quickly discover two facts:

1) The only natural form of change is decay—this means organized change is *unnatural*, and
2) Systems fight hard for stability—this means change will *always face resistance*.

To suggest that change need only be *managed* neglects the inevitable forces of sabotage which seek to undermine transformation and re-balance the system towards the decaying familiar.

Change or Stability, Never Both

At the height of cold-war funding, NASA partnered with the Grumman Corporation to develop a forward swept-wing aircraft. The problem was that the natural stability of an aft-swept wing drew the airflow towards the tip of the wing where there was the least control in counteracting the natural stability of the airfoil. Sharp maneuverable angles of attack were impossible with traditional wing mounting because the plane would naturally return to level flight.

As early as the 1930's German engineers experimented with forward swept-wing designs. Wind tunnel simulations of the design confirmed this "backward-wing" position provided amazing maneuverability as the air-flow was forced inwards toward the controlling ailerons rather than outward toward the wing-tips. At the time, however, light-weight construction materials which could withstand the tremendous torsional forces did not exist; only a few prototypes (JU-287) were ever constructed.

By the late 1970's such materials had been developed and the X-29A was completed in 1984. The X-29A demonstrated excellent control and maneuvering qualities at an angle of attack up to 45 degrees. There was also a decrease in turbulence. However, the wing configuration made the craft inherently unstable. It could fly only with constant corrections to the shape of the airfoil (up to 40 per second) provided by the computerized flight control system. The system was made up of three redundant digital computers backed up by three redundant analog computers. Any of the three systems could fly it on its own, but the redundancy allowed them to check for errors. Each of the three would computationally "vote" on their measurements, so that if one was malfunctioning its contradictory feedback could be detected. Such redundancy meant that a total failure of the system was as unlikely as that of a conventional aircraft, but the expense required to compensate for the X-29A's natural instability made production impractical. The entire project was scuttled by 1992.

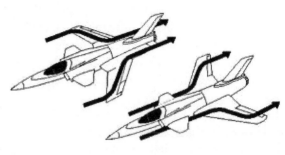

Leaders in a changing organization experience the same forces confronting an aeronautical engineer. On the one hand stable flight is safe and efficient. Commercial jetliners are designed to fly level and smooth. The greatest amount of pilot attention and fuel are consumed when the aircraft is fighting the stability intended by its design, times like takeoff, landing, and turns. At these times, preferably planned, the crew pays particular attention to the feedback systems of the aircraft. During the majority of the flight, once cruising altitude is obtained, the crew is permitted the luxury of doing just that—cruising.

Well-established institutions are designed for cruising. Their production, reporting, and auditing all align for maximum stability. Throughout the organization's cycle there are predictable moments of transition, seasonal adjustments, leadership transfers, and resource cycles. While these periods of transition may require greater attention from the "crew", policies and procedures function like flight checklists; they have been designed to limit the need for improvisation. Predictable changes to the organization's steady functioning are nothing more than routine takeoffs or landings.

As with the flight-plan of a commercial airliner, aggressive or defensive maneuvers are seldom necessary in stable organizations, and therefore are rarely part of the "craft's" design. If a sudden shift in the organization's performance is required due to outside influences like changing demographics, competition, or new markets, or by internal forces which challenge the integrity of the organization, then the same forces which once kept the organization aloft suddenly threaten to tear the structure apart.

Lead *through* Change—Look Back and Look Forward

When Moses died Joshua faced a unique opportunity. A nation with a forty-year history of nomadic stability needed to change if the children of Israel were to conquer the Promised Land. For Joshua, recent history was not on his side. These were descendents of slaves who up until the weeks before the Exodus found their ethnic identity to be a mark of humiliation and subservience. Pharaoh, who had controlled their every move, "knew not Joseph" (Exodus 1:8). In the confines of the slave ghetto instruction regarding any "Promised Land" was repressed.

Change is not managed. It is prepared for, it is fostered, it is inflicted—it is willed! Change is not natural to our human condition. We are designed, programmed, and equipped for the *status quo*. We are keyed for the predictable, conditioned for the familiar. People are not *managed* through change, they are *led through it.*

Inspiring change requires leaders to identify resonant characteristics which convey how the *true* identity of the congregation can only be fulfilled through change. A people become what they *must* become only when their leaders counter their natural resistance to change with a vision of their identity that makes change necessary for them to remain consistent. Transformation requires leaders to understand and step towards the fullness of what has been prophetically taught, to see the future not as possibility, but as a mandate to transform the people into who they are destined to be.

When Joshua took command he seized on a small window of opportunity. He wasted no time in shifting the orientation of the entire nation. Rather than battling structures and attitudes of stable nomadic cruising, Joshua highlighted the people's past and appealed to their inevitable future. Their historic identity was found in the Ancient Covenant; their future was found in the Law of Moses.

The Ancient Covenant with Abraham, Isaac, and Jacob was a promise of land. Joshua continually spoke of this land as the true identity of the people. At the same time the Law of Moses was a codification for a settled people, not a guidebook for nomadic tribes. Joshua's brilliance was to highlight the dissonance between the people's present reality as complacent tent-dwellers with their ideal purpose, both past and future, as a homeland people. This identity was at the core of both Covenant and Law.

Throughout the Exodus, "into the land" was a repeated cadence (Exodus 3:17, 13:5, 13:11, 23:23, Num 13:27, 14:16, 14:24, 20:12, 32:7, Deut 2:29, 6:10, 7:1, 9:28, 11:29, 27:2, 31:7, 20, 21, and 23). This phrase became the battle cry of Commander Joshua.

The stakes were high. If Moses had been constantly thwarted by the romantic safety of slavery, Joshua's resistance was the familiarity of the wilderness.

Joshua was able to lead the children of Israel across the river, through the battles, and into the Promised Land because he appealed to their past and future identity. As nomads they were nothing more than children of a dream, a people of a wish, or inheritors of a myth. But if they succeeded their true identity would be confirmed. With success their resources, their sweat, and their blood would be redeemed by a transformed reality.

What the people knew of themselves as freedmen was learned from scratch. While there may have been accounts of Abraham and Sarah, Isaac and Rebecca, and Jacob and Rachael handed down from generation to generation, these were little more than fireside tales which highlighted how obviously un-chosen their present condition seemed to be.

The living memory of the people provided no resource for institutional maneuverability. The apparatus put in place by Moses was for a nomadic people seeking pastureland, not a warrior nation seeking conquest. In tents and tabernacles the community had become familiar with wilderness living. Even religion took place in a portable building.

Forty years in the wilderness did little to change the people's self perception. One-by-one those who had fled slavery died in the desert. For the first generation, "into the land" was something they would never experience. Even Moses, the great liberator and lawgiver, was buried in an unmarked grave in the unpromising soil beneath the shadow of Mt. Nebo. If Joshua were to find success, he would do so against the torsional forces of nomadic stability.

Lead *through* Change or Allow Division to Stagnate

Forty years before, when Moses returned to Egypt fresh from his Spirit-in-the-shrub encounter, YHWH instructed him to meet first with the elders of the children of Israel (Exodus 3:16-20). When Moses and Aaron announced to the people that God had heard their misery and they would be liberated, news of the possibility of change resulted in sudden enthusiasm (Exodus 4: 29-31).

Until that moment, these descendents of Abraham were a people with no positive experience corresponding to their identity. They knew who they were because their Egyptian slave masters told them. And now, because Moses announced liberation, their hearts stirred with hope.

A funny thing happens to enthusiasm when it confronts the hard work of change—it evaporates.

In Exodus 5, Moses, bolstered by the backing of the people, approached Pharaoh asking for a few days off for a religious retreat into the desert. Pharaoh, not a little nervous over the sheer number of Israelites, denied the request. To allow the children of Israel to wander off in the desert for a little soul-searching and team-building could be devastating. As far as Pharaoh was concerned, the less they grouped together the better.

Strategically, Pharaoh made a good call. Not only does he deny them leave of absence, he increases the Israelite's workload by making them responsible for straw-acquisition at the brick kilns. No longer would the Egyptians gather the straw and deliver it. Now the Israelites would need to go out into the fields, collect the straw, and haul it to the brickyard. And, "By the way," said Pharaoh, "the production quotas remain unchanged!" (Exodus 5:10-14).

Pharaoh accomplished two things with this edict. First, he more widely scattered the slaves. In the straw fields, conversations about identity and possibility would be difficult. Previously confined to the brick factory, the Israelite workers could talk to one another because they worked side-by-side. The IBEBW (Israelite Brotherhood of Egyptian Brick Workers) could organize in the camaraderie of shared labor. When Pharaoh divided them into straw-gatherers and brick-makers, part of the team was spread into the fields with no contact.

This little management lesson demonstrates one way to sabotage change—undermine communication by making the people spread out.

As a consultant I've witnessed congregational subgroups actively sabotage change: early-service verses late-service, single adult verses young couples, or chancel choir verses praise team. The more decentralized an organization the easier it is to sabotage change.

A large urban congregation I attended installed a new senior pastor in the 11:00 Sunday Morning service. His installation came after an international search. The service was magnificent and the tone of the congregation seemed uniformly enthusiastic. That evening I was to meet with a young-adult fellowship group, so I remained throughout the day sitting in as an observer for a number of mission, study, and committee meetings. One fellowship group, which targeted senior singles (fifty and over), served a light supper prior to the evening service. I was invited to share dinner.

While enjoying soup and sandwiches, I overheard several people talking about the wonderful installation service held that morning, but unlike the other groups in the congregation there was a note of apprehension about the new leader. "You know," said one woman, "[The new pastor] has absolutely no interest in the seniors, for him it's all about the youth—young people, young people, young people, that's all he's concerned about. We're going to have to pull together if we're going to survive!"

The new senior pastor had been in his position for less than six hours and already he was a perceived threat!

After some research into the pastoral-search process, I discovered the then-candidate had not met with this particular fellowship group, nor did they have any representation or contact with the search committee. The oversight was neither intentional nor detrimental in the long run, but it does illustrate how uneven communication across divided constituencies results in quick dissension.

Pharaoh instinctively understood the power of division. If he could get the Israelites divided in both location and task, and then add to the fatigue of their workload, their power to unify would unravel.

But the second impact of Pharaoh's decision served to drive a wedge between the people and their new leader, Moses. All the enthusiasm expressed at the end of Exodus chapter 4 disappeared by the end of chapter 5.

> **The Israelite foremen realized they were in trouble when they were told, "You are not to reduce the number of bricks required of you for each day." When they left Pharaoh, they found Moses and Aaron waiting to meet them, and they said, "May the LORD look upon you and judge you! You have made us a stench to Pharaoh and his officials and have put a sword in their hand to kill us." (Exodus 5:19-21)**

Then, all too characteristically, Moses loses confidence to bring about change.

> **Moses returned to the LORD and said, "O Lord, why have you brought trouble upon this people? Is this why you sent me? Ever since I went to Pharaoh to speak in your name, he has brought trouble upon this people, and you have not rescued your people at all." (5:22-23)**

God responds to Moses in Exodus 6 telling him the people would be liberated and he would lead them out of bondage, but the rift was too great. Moses not only had an enemy in Pharaoh, the people also turned against him. Moses used this division as a reason to predict failure.

> Moses reported this to the Israelites, but they did not listen to him because of their discouragement and cruel bondage.
>
> Then the LORD said to Moses, "Go, tell Pharaoh King of Egypt to let the Israelites go out of his country."
>
> But Moses said to the LORD, "If the Israelites will not listen to me, why would Pharaoh listen to me, since I speak with faltering lips?" (Exodus 6:9-12)

What happened became an unfortunate pattern for Moses' leadership with the children of Israel. Time and again when things got tough, the people turned on Moses threatening to go back to Egypt and the familiarity of slavery. Moses, in turn, would complain to God questioning the purpose and possibility of his calling.

Moses' problem was his self-perception as a "change-manager". Believing that the desire for transformation from slavery to freedom would arise naturally from the people, Moses spent most of his time preparing operating manuals for a new order. But all the pages of law were of no use when Moses faced the reality of a resistant people. The capacity to defend the familiar, even when it stinks, is stunningly powerful when people are confronted with the hard work of change.

Lead *through* Change or Settle for a Short-Term Quick-Fix

Change leaders must prepare to be sabotaged by the very *status quo* they wish to transform. No matter how much ground-work, team-building, or pledged-support they have prior to change, most of it will disappear as the organization wrestles for a return to the familiar. Understanding this fact prior to change is crucial if a leader is to lead *through* change.

Working with student-seminarians and new pastors I am often asked, "When is the best time to make change?" Some organizational coaches suggest that leaders wait until they have spent some time learning the *status quo*, building alliances, and winning the trust of the community. Others suggest that change best occurs during the "honey-moon" period, the early days of leadership when people anticipate difference.

When is the best time to make change? It is when the leadership is personally prepared to endure the sabotage that will inevitably accompany their efforts.

Leaders must be prepared for crisis. But there is a difference between managing crises from external threats and facing crisis created by internal resistance. It is axiomatic—the greatest threats come from within.

Internal crisis is most often the consequence of incoherent or inconsistent movement towards change. This is true at every level of the organization. No matter how effectively the leadership trains or delegates members of a congregation, never mind how many announcements have been printed in the newsletter, don't be fooled by the conversations at committee meetings, if change is attempted in the context of an incoherent corporate environment, crises will erupt.

In Exodus 32 Moses is standing in the serious, somber, smoky, reality of God's law-giving presence. Meanwhile Aaron prepares to party.

Up to this point, other than a few showy miracles for Pharaoh's court and the plagues visited on the Egyptians, the Israelites had little opportunity to know anything about their identity as a people or their YHWH-God. Without a coherent understanding of themselves, they wanted gods like everybody else. After all, gods told you what was important. Like a mission statement, gods give people priorities, purpose, and plans. The rhythm of the days, the reasons for celebrations, and the seasons for sacrifice are defined by the gods.

Here at camp Sinai, the people knew virtually nothing regarding their patron Deity. They grew frustrated. Egyptians had their sun god and the divinity of the Nile. Those in the desert had bovine deities delivering water, food, companionship, and fertility. Everybody else had a picture or a statue of their gods, but the children of Israel had nothing. Besides, not only was the Israelite God unwilling to show any self-representation, this YHWH-God was connected to a land the people had never seen.

No longer slaves, they were now wanderers. No longer linked to the rhythms of flood, planting, and harvest, they were tethered to the wanderings of livestock. Sitting around at the bottom of a mountain, who were they? What were they doing? And how were they to express their identity, purpose, and place in a wilderness? And so, where the subsistence of life relied on good grazing land for milk production, why not bow down to a big-eyed shiny calf-god?

Meanwhile, Moses was off receiving blueprints for the Ark of the Covenant, the Tabernacle and its furniture. Written versions of YHWH's Covenant with Abraham had not yet been distributed, and the commandments and laws were still in their first draft. Absent a second commandment regarding graven images, the people saw little reason to stall any longer. They simply did what people do—they constructed a god in the image of their need.

Amazingly Aaron was all too willing to write off his little brother.

> When the people saw that Moses was so long in coming down from the mountain, they gathered around Aaron and said, "Come, make us gods who will go before us. As for this fellow Moses who brought us up out of Egypt, we don't know what has happened to him."
>
> Aaron answered them, "Take off the gold earrings that your wives, your sons and your daughters are wearing, and bring them to me." So all the people took off their earrings and brought them to Aaron. He took what they handed him and made it into an idol cast in the shape of a calf, fashioning it with a tool. Then they said, "These are your gods, O Israel, who brought you up out of Egypt."
>
> When Aaron saw this, he built an altar in front of the calf and announced, "Tomorrow there will be a festival to the LORD." So the next day the people rose early and sacrificed burnt offerings and presented fellowship offerings. Afterward they sat down to eat and drink and got up to indulge in revelry. (Exodus 32:1-6)

What made Aaron so spineless? There is absolutely no protest from the big brother of Moses. Why does Aaron assume his little brother was dead? This was the same little brother who, as an infant, was saved from Pharaoh's slaughter, who fled to the land of the Midianites to avoid a murder rap, who came back to challenge Pharaoh to his face, who called down the plagues, and divided the Red Sea. But now little brother Moses is delayed on his camping trip with YHWH, and Aaron quickly accepts the assertion that he is dead. There's no moment for mourning, just plans for a party.

Like a teenager plotting a blowout as soon as the parents are out-of-town, Aaron rolls up his sleeves, ready to do whatever the crowd suggests. They want a god of their very own, formed in the likeness of their current desire. No problem. Pass the plates, build the forge, drop in the jewelry, fashion the gold—in two short verses Aaron provides one ready-made calf-god for the indulgent service of the people. Big brother Aaron then calls for a festival in complete dishonor of the absent Moses.

(Perhaps this is why it is difficult for senior executives to use all of their vacation. Could a few days away for a conference spell the complete unraveling of a life's work?)

As Moses and Joshua returned to the Israelite encampment, a great noise was coming from the people. Joshua, who clearly had a taste for battle, assumed the commotion was another military ambush. Running down the side of the mountain, the adrenalin-rush pushed Joshua's mind to strategies for defense.

> "When Joshua heard the noise of the people shouting,
> he said to Moses, 'There is the sound of war in the
> camp!'" (Exodus 32:17)

Moses on the other hand, brought up in the frat-house world of an Egyptian prince, knew the sound of a party when he heard one.

> "Moses replied:
> 'It is not the sound of victory,
> it is not the sound of defeat;
> it is the sound of singing that I hear.'"
> (Exodus 32:18)

In a way, however, Joshua was correct. While the sound was singing, the torment in the camp was warfare. A battle was being waged for the future of a people. Were the people to wait in quiet anticipation of a God linked to a land they had never seen and promised to ancestors who generations before moved to Egypt? Or were the children of Israel going to settle for a nomadic existence complete with tribute to their temporary aspirations? Since the days of Joseph they had resided in foreign country, now they were finally going home. But "home" was a foreign land so very far away. Why not just settle here?

Effective leaders are constantly battling the short-cut temptation of incomplete gods. The children of Israel were just like us, easily seduced by the empty promises of an idolatrous quick-fix. Moving toward an unseen goal requires patience, diligence, and delayed gratification. It is not only difficult, it is unnatural.

Deities at hand promise rapid ease and pleasant outcomes. We are tempted to hedge our bets, toss a few resources towards the short-term goals, throw a party, toast our success, and become like everybody else.

It is all too human to make gods which match the aspirations of our immediate need. Idolatry does not elevate human desire; desire shapes our idols. Agricultural societies sacrifice to the rain and the fertility of the earth. Seafaring communities bear homage to wind and fish. Nomadic tribes bow down to calves. Idols permit us to worship only what we need and sacrifice only for what we desire.

This is why throughout the Hebrew Scriptures the calf-god remained particularly repugnant. Calf-gods were for herders—peripatetic people detached for the land, bound by clan, fresh water, and ever-changing grassland. To worship the calf would concretize their identity as wanderers, wilderness-dwellers tied to no specific place, perpetually on the move, chasing always after baby cows.

But the descendents of Israel were not liberated from Egyptian slavery to become wanderers. The purpose of the Exodus was not to end slavery and create a new alliance of nomadic tribes. The children of Israel were called out of Egypt to take possession of a Promised Land. The Abrahamic Covenant was specific—it was a land, a place, a nation. For the children of Israel to nuzzle up to a calf-god would stop them short of the full Covenant.

The point of the plagues, the Passover, the parting sea, the cloud, the fire, the smoke, the manna, the quail, the water from the rock, etc., was to sustain them until they claimed their inheritance. To be distracted by nomadic values denies the single purpose for which they journeyed.

Joshua was right. The sound of singing was the evidence of Aaron's surrender. Warfare had begun!

Lead *through* Change or Build Your Crisis Management Skills

Moses, who understood something of the big picture, was disgusted. Unfortunately all that was left for the moment was crisis intervention.

> **19** When Moses approached the camp and saw the calf and the dancing, his anger burned and he threw the tablets out of his hands, breaking them to pieces at the foot of the mountain. **20** And he took the calf they had made and burned it in the fire; then he ground it to powder, scattered it on the water and made the Israelites drink it.

> **21** He said to Aaron, "What did these people do to you, that you led them into such great sin?"

> **22** "Do not be angry, my lord," Aaron answered. "You know how prone these people are to evil. **23** They said to me, 'Make us gods who will go before us. As for this fellow Moses who brought us up out of Egypt, we don't know what has happened to him.' **24** So I told them, 'Whoever has any gold jewelry, take it off.' Then they

gave me the gold, and I threw it into the fire, and out came this calf!"

25 Moses saw that the people were running wild and that Aaron had let them get out of control and so become a laughingstock to their enemies. **26** So he stood at the entrance to the camp and said, "Whoever is for the LORD, come to me." And all the Levites rallied to him.

27 Then he said to them, "This is what the LORD, the God of Israel, says: 'Each man strap a sword to his side. Go back and forth through the camp from one end to the other, each killing his brother and friend and neighbor.'"**28** The Levites did as Moses commanded, and that day about three thousand of the people died. **29** Then Moses said, "You have been set apart to the LORD today, for you were against your own sons and brothers, and he has blessed you this day."

30 The next day Moses said to the people, "You have committed a great sin. But now I will go up to the LORD; perhaps I can make atonement for your sin." (Exodus 32:19-30)

Arriving at the base of Mt. Sinai, Moses witnesses a spectacle of apostate distraction; he is furious! After all, he is working on their behalf; he has nothing but their best interest at heart. And, as so many insecure change-managers do, Moses shifts into crisis-management mode.

The same impulsivity that got Moses into trouble when he killed the Egyptian, served him well in crisis. Moses' action at the foot of Sinai provides an impressive guide to end crisis effectively, swiftly, and completely. The impact of Moses crisis intervention is clear; the people would never again build an idol on Moses' watch.

The text provides four-steps for crisis intervention:

1) Moses drops what he was doing—quite literally, smashing the first draft of the Law (verse 19).
2) Moses thoroughly removes the focal point of the rebellion—burning the calf, grinding it into powder, and making the people drink their mistake (verse 20).

3) Moses reestablishes order:
   a) He identifies loyal assistants (verses 25 & 26).
   b) Moves quickly to get the people's attention. With an immediate downsizing by 3,000, he quickly silences the opposition (verses 27 & 28).
   c) Moses then rewards his enforcers (verse 29).
4) Moses then publicly rebukes those responsible and returns to his work, walking back up the mountain to get the second copy of the law (verse 30).

When Moses calls upon the Levites to put down the insurrection at Camp Sinai they respond efficiently. But up to that moment, the people had functioned without a clue. Even the Levites had participated in calf-building; as a result they had to slaughter some of their own to regain order. The text blames the crisis on the impatience of the people, but Moses and Aaron share some responsibility for the apostasy.

When leadership is weak, crisis intervention is all leaders can do. "Things may not be going well," they argue, "but dadgummit I'm not going to allow things to go backwards!" Without the establishment of order, discipline, and integrity, the time and energy of the leaders is spent "putting out fires".

Moses' decisive action worked profoundly well at the foot of Mt Sinai—it put an end to the foolishness; but the determination and drive employed by Moses in times of crisis was seldom seen in times of calm. Even after this moment of action Moses' style doesn't change. His continual response to the resistance of the people alternated between impulsive outbursts and selfish brooding. Whenever the people complain, Moses grows angry and whines to God who provides some miracle, sign, or punishment, forcing the people into compliance until the next crisis.

The people settled too easily for a calf-god partially because Moses never grasped his true authority, and so he was unable to lead the people to their final destination. For the next four decades Moses remained self-doubting and wavering in his conviction as a leader.

Doubtless, Joshua took note. Joshua witnessed Moses smashing the tablets of the law, grinding the Golden Calf into a bitter medicine, sending the Levites as riot police, and slaughtering 3,000 in the name of crowd control. Joshua saw the quick, strategic, and effective response by Moses. Joshua saw Moses' disgust over the Golden Calf, the dithering response of Aaron, and the exuberant celebration of the people, all fueling Moses' rage. But in the long run, Joshua saw how rage failed improve Moses' capacity to lead.

On his second trip up Sinai Moses ascended to retrieve a back-up copy of the law, Joshua did not come along. Instead he remained at the meeting-tent. There Joshua could kept a closer eye on the assembly and perhaps lend some back-bone to the all too pliable Aaron (Exodus 33:11).

Lead *through* Change by Sharing Outcomes Not Goals

We live in a post-denominational age, a time of profound change for the context of the Christian Church. Once upon a time the traditional divisions of creed and content defined American Protestantism. Rite flowed from theological understanding and congregational identity was rooted in a connection to tradition based on denominational identity.

In a denominational time what you believed, more than anything else, defined how you worshipped. Confirmation and membership classes were taught in catechetical form. New converts and reaffirming members were required to articulate their faith as either an intellectual ascent to a set of beliefs, or the affirmation of a particular religious experience.

As a new parish pastor, I had anticipated theological content and religious experience to be of primary importance to the members of my congregation. That was not the case. This is not to say that members and perspective members disdained the content of the tradition, it just held no practical relevance. They treated theological information as one would approach answers for the popular board game "Trivial Pursuits"—something worth knowing only for its novelty. A comprehensive understanding of the tradition's creeds and confessions was of little importance. Congregational identity had nothing to do with denominationalism, theological heritage, or religious experience. Other factors, such as the building's architecture, the congregation's age, or the members' ethnicity articulated their identity far more powerfully than theological ideals or doctrinal interpretation.

We were the church across the street from the Methodists, down the hill from the Baptists, and three blocks from the Roman Catholics (in two directions!). Our primary difference from these other congregations was that we were racially integrated, we still had a few young people, and, of greatest importance to the elderly members, we were NOT Irish. The fact we were Presbyterian was of far less significance then the fact that we had a parking lot (something few Protestant congregations in our Chicago neighborhood could boast).

My initial pastoral response to this reality was to convey the content of the tradition with aggressive zeal. I offered classes—most of them well attended—on the history of the Reformed Tradition, the background of our Creeds and Confessions, the importance of Presbyterian Polity, and, of course, the scriptures, both Old and New Testaments. I firmly believed that the members needed this information to function more effectively as a Presbyterian congregation. We had a particular character as Presbyterians and I hoped the members would find cohesiveness as a people connected by the tenants of their heritage. I believed denominational identity rooted in theological tradition would transcend issues of location, gender, class, age, race, and maybe even parking.

Seven years into my pastorate, I felt I was beginning to make headway. The elders attended training classes, confirmation graduates were able to identify the documents found in our Creeds and Confessions, and even the Deacons could articulate their role in relationship to the church's Elder Board and Trustees.

Then, one evening during our informal Wednesday worship service, one of our elders, who had been a Presbyterian most of her adult life, commented, "Sometimes I think I am a denomination of one. No one else seems to see the world or believe like I do." Before I could respond or ask any questions, another elder responded, "I know exactly what you mean. I really don't think I feel connected to what other people believe." As I looked around the room I saw several heads nodding in agreement.

What was going on? These were people informed by the past years of classes and discussions. These were among the most active participants in the educational programs of the church. Had they secretly been harboring heresy and now were confessing their divergence with church doctrine? Were we about to embark on a series of investigations to discern the orthodoxy of the congregation's leadership?

Over the next several weeks I attempted to find out what these individuals meant by their sense of theological isolation. My motivation was not church discipline, but a hope to understand what the members actually believed. As their pastor, I had some knowledge of how they behaved; it was a small congregation. I knew who could be counted on to volunteer for activities, I knew who would contribute to which program, I was well aware of which members were not speaking to each other, and I even knew a little about who had offended whom. But *what* they believed? Their inner understanding and deepest passions remained a deep mystery.

This discovery troubled me. Belief and theological understanding did not guide my members. While they could now articulate the elements of the tradition, there was no connection between the words of doctrine and the ordering of their lives. What made them *tick* was not an affirmation of content, but the interplay between feeling and fellowship. Loyalty to the church was driven not by the desire to articulate a Presbyterian and Reformed way-of-being, but by a commitment borne of shared experience with a group of familiar faces. Attachment for any particular individual to the congregational body could be interpreted by the degree to which that person saw his or her life experiences overlap with the experiences of others in the congregation.

The participants in Wednesday worship shared their sense of isolation not because they held a set of unshared theological interpretations; instead they were speaking a deep longing to feel more connected. Their daily experience had little or nothing to do with their fellow members. The few short hours they spent each week within the same religious space connected them to the other members only for that time, and only in relationship to a religious corporation. They sensed no cohesive intimacy extending beyond the walls of our building. This was in tension with what *I* thought to be important.

I was trained in academic theology; I believed the content of the tradition should be the glue of the community. I discovered instead how theological identity was as mercurial as political affiliation. With few exceptions, the congregation cared far less about *what I believed* than *how I treated* them. I interpreted their concern as shallow—a mindset which nearly destroyed my ability to pastor.

When I discovered the congregation's disinterest in big ideas, I became despondent. If they weren't interested in better theological understanding, then perhaps I was the wrong pastor; the first six years of my ministry had been in vain. I was, as one member put it, "in a funk". My preaching became judgmental, my teaching became condescending, and my effectiveness sunk to an all-time low.

Fortunately for the congregation, my descent into disgust was short-lived. As it turned out, I really did care about these people. As I continued my routine of hospital visitation, baptisms, funerals, and pastoral care, I slowly refocused my energy toward an emotional connection to the congregation. All those years of teaching were important not because members better grasped theological concepts, but because they were treated as people who mattered. They mattered so much that I asked them to think.

The content of the classes, discussions, and preaching was not as crucial as the tone I struck in presentation. When members were treated with dignity, I was given their attention. But when I trivialized their capacity to share my passion, my ministry was devastated. The importance of maintaining theological integrity was *my* issue, not theirs. I passionately conveyed this priority because *I* believed it was important, but it was the *passion* that engaged the members not the content.

The trump of passion over content explained why various programs worked and others failed. Stewardship, youth, worship, and retreats were a hit or a bust based not on programmatic content, but on the leaders' respect for the participants.

The issue was not qualification, tradition, or charisma. While some events could be launched by the draw of personality or expectation, sustained collective energy was only possible through a passionate commitment to results, shared by both leaders and members.

The congregation I served struggled in a neighborhood filled with racism, ethnic tension, and class anxiety. In light of these struggles, the congregation flourished not because I told them the *right* way to understand; change occurred because within the fellowship of the congregation, they found a unifying passion. My commitment to the theological issues and doctrinal detail was necessary to keep *me* on track. This commitment maintained my dedication to the integrity of our work.

The goal of theological sophistication did not engage the congregation; but the shared outcome of passion and mutual respect unified a diverse community.

Had I continued to insist the congregation share my goal of theological comprehension, they would have disintegrated. The issue was not shared goals. Contrary to popular assumptions about organizational change, leaders and members need not own identical goals. What is necessary is that both leaders and members desire similar outcomes even if they gather for divergent purposes.

The congregation did not share my obsession with understanding Presbyterianism. They did, however, share a passion to participate and learn. My goal was to effectively convey the content of the tradition; the congregation's goal was to participate in something important. We were meeting different goals, but celebrated identical outcomes. This created an unmistakable bond.

This was the powerful element of leadership that allowed Joshua to lead through change. Joshua's passion for the people drove their allegiance even when they did not completely understand the outcome.

For Joshua, as for all change leaders, three elements are requirements for change: connectivity, clarity, and continuity.

Lead *through* Change by Connecting to the Congregation

As Rabbi Edwin Freidman once said in a lecture, "When you spill something on someone at a party, the reaction is proportional to your prior relationship with the person, not the size of the stain." A few drops of club soda on a dark dress will elicit great hostility from your enemy, but a whole glass of cranberry juice spilled on the white suit of a close friend is dismissed as a humorous *faux pas*.

Joshua understood the principle of connectivity. From the beginning of his administration inclusivity was Joshua's unyielding passion. In taking command,

Joshua understood that only a tribal federation could conquer the Promised Land. Military and political victory required unity.

As the book of Joshua opens, the Reubenites, Gadites, and the half tribe of Manasseh are already home. Joshua needed to convince these tribes to cross with him. Without them the nation could not win. The power of his first speech as full commander is a rousing call to connectivity in which he appeals to tradition, reason, and courage.

> . . . To the Reubenites, the Gadites and the half-tribe of Manasseh, Joshua said, "Remember the command that Moses the servant of the LORD gave you: 'The LORD your God is giving you rest and has granted you this land.' Your wives, your children and your livestock may stay in the land that Moses gave you east of the Jordan, but all your fighting men, fully armed, must cross over ahead of your brothers. You are to help your brothers until the LORD gives them rest, as he has done for you, and until they too have taken possession of the land that the LORD your God is giving them. After that, you may go back and occupy your own land, which Moses the servant of the LORD gave you east of the Jordan toward the sunrise." (Joshua 1:12-15)

Joshua declared that no one would be "home" until everybody was "home". If the confederation of twelve tribes fought together, the possibility of victory was in reach. If, as each territory was claimed, the tribes peeled-off to their possession, by the time they arrived at the land of the 12th tribe, the remaining army would be too small to accomplish the task.

The principle of connectivity is crucial for organizational change. This is why motivational speakers provide great entertainment but seldom lasting change.

When a new pastor arrives, she or he is afforded a great deal of latitude in decision making. In this period, referred to as the "honeymoon", new ideas are embraced, dynamic programs are introduced, and approval ratings remain high. Over time, however, the new leader is given less slack; change once welcomed is now resisted. Even simple changes which would previously occur without discussion become points of hostility and conflict.

This can lead to self-doubt on the part of the minister, resulting in questions ranging from the appropriateness of his or her placement, to the possibility that he or she may not even be called to ministry.

What happens is not a deterioration of skill on the part of the minister or the sudden immergence of previously benign disagreement in the congregation, but the sudden recognition that the leader is now "connected".

Previously there was no emotional interdependence or intimacy between the pastor and the congregation. The change was being proposed by a stranger who was afforded the respect of an outside expert. The congregation forgave any "ignorance" regarding the impact of change because the pastor was new. He or she could not be aware of the impact of each and every decision. Over time, however, active ministry brings connection. Eventually the pastor is no longer afforded the long-leash of ignorance. Crucial at this point is the leader's ability to connect to the people's deeper identity. Familiarity must orient the leader toward an identity beyond current circumstances.

When Joshua announced the people's collective responsibility, the Promise to the Patriarchs had been taught for only a generation. Joshua moved their understanding of Covenant from ancient oath to current event.

This transition connected these stable nomads to an identity as maneuverable warriors. This became possible because Joshua was oriented toward their newly infused yet ancient identity. The very Law of Moses implied that the wilderness was not their purpose. The constitutive documents of the nation declared the elements necessary, inspiring the people to risk energy, time, resources, will, and life. Within *The Law* was *The Promise*.

Lead *through* Change by Clarifying Identity

In the face of unbelievable odds, Joshua's command became possible and sustainable because he insisted change was necessary if the people were to remain connected to their identity. If they did not fight for change, they would lose their purpose.

Stable organizations can be led through catastrophic times if the core of their identity contains prophetic possibility. But leaders must be constantly aware that transformation is not without significant cost.

Requiring a stable craft to flex like a fighter-plane will threaten to rend it to the breaking point. Significant transitions are possible only if they are rooted in core identity, and teaching that identity can only occur during times of stability.

Too often stagnation becomes the identity of an organization. The costs of change are perceived to be overwhelming because change is seen as a loss of identity. If change means only loss, it will be resisted at all cost. But if change is understood as movement toward a fuller expression of identity, then *stagnation* becomes the greatest liability.

While serving a congregation undergoing the stress of racial transition, I discovered just how catastrophic change could be perceived to be. It had been nearly fifteen years since the first African-American families had joined the congregation. The initial hemorrhage of white families had been stalled through near heroic efforts on the part of a previous pastor. By his tireless visitation, members maintained a personal loyalty to their pastor. But members found little commitment to an integrated community; that identity had not been taught.

The traditional wisdom of both the congregation and the denomination was that mono-racial congregations were the only viable form of community. It was deeply believed that in a matter of time the congregation would re-segregate as all-black or disintegrate and close.

Only after I had accepted the call did I discover the denomination had identified our congregation for closure. Prior to my arrival interim reports to the local office indicated that there was no will among the white members for inclusion of blacks. What I further discovered was that even the African-American members who had joined the church were told that they were somehow insufficiently loyal to their ethnic identity because they were willing to join a majority white church. Such thinking placed ethnic identity in a position which was more powerful than congregational identity. With this view there was no way to overcome the cultural forces requiring the congregation to become one thing or another.

Attempts by an interim pastor to "re-brand" the congregation as "more black" not only failed, but looked ridiculous. (There is something pathetic about watching elderly white members endure "gospel fests", while eyeing their black counterparts with suspicion, as if the calls for awkward hand-clapping and holy dancing were *their* fault.) In seeking a "more black" identity, changes to worship style were adopted to appeal to people who were *not* present in the congregation. When innovation failed, the interim pastor blamed the people.

In one conversation with my interim predecessor, I was told the church was going to die because they did not capture the power of *his* prophetic ministry.

In sharing this conversation with a seasoned African-American pastor in the community, he suggested the problem wasn't in the pews but in the pulpit. He reminded me that the focus of ministry must always be "the hearts and lives of the congregation God gives you on Sunday, not the folk who don't show up." Wisely, he gave me the advice, "If you think you're leading, and nobody is following, you're just taking a walk!"

Over time I realized the majority of the congregation was not equipped for transition because they had been told the only way their church could survive was for them to leave. This oxymoronic identity was becoming a self-fulfilling prophecy. Members saw themselves as either killing the church by resisting change, or allowing the church to grow by leaving. As an organization, the congregation became powerfully passive-aggressive; never getting behind innovation while doggedly defending the *status quo*.

For me the reality became snapshot-clear when we hired a new custodian. For a part-time, minimum-wage position we had received no less than 22 applications. Only one white applicant was in the interview pool, an elderly gentleman who had suffered a stroke and could not use his right arm. Needless to say he was not my first choice for the position. I hired a young African-American man with stellar references and extensive experience in building maintenance. His full-time work schedule permitted exactly the flexibility we required; I felt lucky to hire him.

I introduced him to the congregation on his first Sunday of employment and, up until that moment, had given no thought to race. That was until I looked out over the congregation to see several angry faces. Following worship when the sanctuary had cleared, one of the chief spokesmen for the "racist opposition" asked me why the church needed so many "coloreds" in positions of authority.

My first reaction was to chuckle, part-time church custodian was hardly "authority" in my mind, and up until that moment I was only grateful to have made a decision. I immediately recognized this was no laughing matter. The parishioner I was facing had clenched fists and a grimaced face. "Minister to the congregation God gives you," echoed in my heart as I readied a response.

"I'm not going to debate this decision, I'm sorry." Somehow God helped me respond. "I don't understand your frustration, and seeing how angry you are I'm not sure I want to understand. But I see you're in lots of pain here, and as your pastor I want to do something about that. This is *your* church and I'm *your* pastor and when I see a member hurting I've got to figure out how to help. But being an integrated congregation is not something I'm going to debate."

The member walked away in disgust, but my recognition of his pain was not forgotten. What mattered was my promise to defend his inclusion in the congregation's future. I *wanted* to be *his* pastor, and at the same time serve an integrated community. I needed to appeal to something greater than race. I believed somewhere in the DNA of the congregation was an identity which would make the hard work of change not only possible, but necessary. Continuity and possibility had to coexist or the congregation would passively or aggressively dissolve.

After careful study of the congregation's history, I discovered several moments of transition. The recent tensions of racial divide had become their identity, but there was a greater and longer history of adaptation. These stories had been forgotten.

At the same time, I had begun a series of sermons on the Book of Joshua. It was there that I discovered how Joshua reclaimed an ancient identity and a future possibility. I saw how this claim galvanized the people. Joshua taught how a congregation's clearest identity was found in its movement, not stagnation—and so they moved.

Lead through Change by Defining Continuity

What became an imperative for my ministry was an education of the members into a deeper identity, a curriculum I needed to build from "scratch".

Hoping the congregation would see their greater purpose as a diverse, inclusive community, I pointed to those moments in their 100-year history when they had weathered several transitions. I began to lift from the archives stories of a congregation embracing change and holding fast to the promise of who they were becoming rather than the stagnation of who they were. In the stories of their own history was the promise of their best selves—a people who could work for hope rather than resist change.

Our movement was made clear in our gradually growing membership. New families visited and stayed because the congregation expressed their hope as an integrated congregation, one which *required* the continued participation of long-standing members, side-by-side with new faces—both black and white. Diversity was *not* the goal it was the consequence of a unity *deeper* than the color of skin. Theirs was a complex identity rooted in the history and heart of *this* Christian community, and I found in that complexity the possibility for unity to continue into its future. The same forces which once threatened to tear the organization apart, were now allowing it to soar to new places.

I did not recognize how far we had come until several years after my encounter with the racist spokesman. I stood beside his hospital bed joining hands while one of our African-American elders said a prayer prior to his surgery. The African-American elder's wife was in the same hospital for surgery that same morning. She was having a lump removed from her breast and while she was in surgery her husband came with me to visit and offer prayer for my white antagonist.

Following prayer we unloosed our hands.

"I understand your wife's having surgery too," said the white member.

Nervous about his wife's condition, the African-American elder said, "Oh it's no big deal, she'll be fine."

"I hope it's not cancer," said the man in the bed, "tell her I'm praying for her. Thanks for praying for me."

I was stunned by how far human hearts had moved, but the full impact of the transition wasn't apparent to me until an hour later when I moved from the recovery room with one member to the preparation room for the other. Coincidently both patients had the same anesthesiologist. Having just seen me with his previous case, a middle-aged African-American woman, the doctor appeared a bit startled to see the same pastor with his next case, an elderly white man.

Before he could acknowledge his surprise, my parishioner highlighted the power of the promise when he said, "Yep, he's my pastor too!"

It was then that I knew how God had maneuvered our little congregation from the wilderness of ethnic tension into the shared land of God's Promise.

CHAPTER V

Evidence of Oriented Leadership—Discipline

The morning after Joshua's encounter with the commander of the army of the LORD was the dawn of a new chapter for The Israelites. They began to possess the Land of Promise, starting with Jericho.

This is one of the most familiar stories in the Bible:

> Now Jericho was tightly shut up because of the Israelites. No one went out and no one came in.
>
> Then the LORD said to Joshua, "See, I have delivered Jericho into your hands, along with its king and its fighting men. March around the city once with all the armed men. Do this for six days. Have seven priests carry trumpets of rams' horns in front of the ark. On the seventh day, march around the city seven times, with the priests blowing the trumpets. When you hear them sound a long blast on the trumpets, have all the people give a loud shout; then the wall of the city will collapse and the people will go up, every man straight in."
>
> So Joshua son of Nun called the priests and said to them, "Take up the ark of the covenant of the LORD and have seven priests carry trumpets in front of it." And he ordered the people, "Advance! March around the city, with the armed guard going ahead of the ark of the LORD."

When Joshua had spoken to the people, the seven priests carrying the seven trumpets before the LORD went forward, blowing their trumpets, and the ark of the LORD's covenant followed them. The armed guard marched ahead of the priests who blew the trumpets, and the rear guard followed the ark. All this time the trumpets were sounding. But Joshua had commanded the people, "Do not give a war cry, do not raise your voices, do not say a word until the day I tell you to shout. Then shout!" So he had the ark of the LORD carried around the city, circling it once. Then the people returned to camp and spent the night there.

Joshua got up early the next morning and the priests took up the ark of the LORD. The seven priests carrying the seven trumpets went forward, marching before the ark of the LORD and blowing the trumpets. The armed men went ahead of them and the rear guard followed the ark of the LORD, while the trumpets kept sounding. So on the second day they marched around the city once and returned to the camp. They did this for six days. (Joshua 6:1-14)

Joshua's orders to his army were straight-forward, "March!" and "Be Quiet!" Straight-forward but not simple. They are the orders of military basic training—six days of silent parade-drill. It was a test of discipline; it was a test of command.

The story clips along quickly. We are given no anecdotes regarding the response of these untested recruits, but anyone who has been in a high school marching band or a 4th of July parade knows how these days unfolded, initially chaotic—eventually ordered. Discipline does not come naturally.

Discipline: Because There is no Manna

As a young pastor I misunderstood the nature of leadership. I believed clarity about facts would generate an automatic response when in reality response to leadership comes through consistent discipline.

The congregation I served was facing financial difficulty. The Treasurer provided regular detailed financial reports which clearly conveyed the congregation's situation, but no one seemed particularly concerned regarding fiscal reality—we were in trouble. I also knew contributions were well below what was possible given the personal assets and income of several members.

I figured that the congregation, and in particular the leadership, merely needed to better understand the facts. Fresh from my position as a computer programmer analyst for the comptroller's office at the university where I had completed graduate school, I felt uniquely qualified to convey the data that would clarify the financial status of the congregation. For the next several days I poured over the congregation's financial records from the past 25 years. I converted the data into straight-forward charts and graphs illustrating the decline in per-household giving adjusted for inflation.

Printing fifteen-page informational packets, I called a joint meeting of the elders and trustees. Using my best presentation skills, I flip-charted (PowerPoint® was not yet available) my way through the clearest, most detailed financial picture I could portray.

At the conclusion of my presentation I looked to my congregation's leadership for a response. In one corner a quiet conversation had begun about the Chicago Bulls, several others were doodling odd pictures on the back of my report, and two or three had nodded off. One trustee had moved his chair closer to the wall so he could clean cobwebs from the baseboard. I asked if there were any questions. Some attention returned to the front of the room.

There were no questions, there was no discussion. An elder made a motion to adjourn which was quickly seconded. The meeting ended. When I received the minutes from the meeting's secretary, they were brief. "Pastor presented a report showing we are in financial trouble. Meeting Adjourned."

It was then I learned that facts move nothing without discipline. Even the most oriented congregation requires discipline to bring about change.

If the walls of Jericho were going to fall as the result of miraculous intervention, why didn't they just collapse? The people could have stumbled around the city, blown their trumpets, shouted a war cry, and by God's great power the walls could have come a tumbelin' down on day one!

But a miraculous quick-fix would have taught nothing to the future fighting force of the Israelites. Before they received the benefit of God's work, they needed to experience discipline.

These fresh recruits had grown up in the unstructured freedom of the wilderness. There the most complicated orders involved chasing sheep and driving cattle to water. In the wilderness bread fell from heaven, but in the Promised Land there was a new reality—a fact they learned in the days before Jericho.

> The day after the Passover, that very day, they ate some of the produce of the land: unleavened bread and roasted grain. The manna stopped the day after they

> ate this food from the land; there was no longer any
> manna for the Israelites. (Joshua 5:11-12a)

Promised Land victory is accomplished without manna.

This is the problem with the Promised Land. No manna falls. Sustenance requires day-by-day mundane drudgery.

In my first congregation, the members had become undisciplined because they had received financial manna for years. At the conclusion of each year my predecessors would quietly call three or four "well-healed" members and inform them of the congregation's financial position. The pastor would then split the deficit among these benefactors and their year-end gifts would balance the budget.

This annual ritual began in the 1940's with a pastor who cultivated these relationships. Upon his retirement in the 1960's he passed the list to his successor who continued the ritual. The subsequent pastor initially rejected the notion of calling on specially cultivated contributors; but a few days after his first Christmas Eve service he received a call from one of these donors who asked how much he needed to settle the year-end balance. The manna that had fallen for more than forty years continued to fall.

By the time I arrived, all the short-list of year-end rescuers had either died or moved to Arizona, but the expectation of a wilderness bail-out was still in place.

One member even asked me if there weren't a handful of members who would just write checks for whatever the general fund needed. When I pointed out these individuals were gone he responded, "Wow, I guess we really *are* in trouble." Yet even his giving habits did not change.

Discipline: Because Data Changes Nothing

Discipline is not inspired by data. It is grown step-by-step, line-by-line, corner-by-corner, day-by-day. A sudden infusion of insight doesn't reform patterns of behavior created by years of emergency bail-outs.

Joshua's army had grown-up on bread from the heavens, low-flying quail, and rocks belching water. They needed to discover both the boredom and benefit of the disciplined march.

Because Jericho is remembered for the final outcome on day seven, it's easy to forget days two though six; undisciplined recruits stomping around in the hot sun, keeping their battle gear on their shoulders, struggling to keep an ordered silence.

The evidence of Joshua's Oriented Leadership was his capacity to maintain discipline through the long-haul.

Leaders may know the importance of the outcome, the urgency of the need, the benefit of cooperative effort, but followers seldom jump into line merely because leaders articulate the obvious.

My first congregation took more than four years of stewardship sermons, newsletter articles, motivational presentations, and discussion of budgets, before broad-based increases in giving began to take hold as the ongoing discipline of the members. I was anxious to jump ahead to the seventh day of the Jericho march, but it took twelve trips around the city before the people witnessed any change.

> On the seventh day, they got up at daybreak and marched around the city seven times in the same manner, except that on that day they circled the city seven times. The seventh time around, when the priests sounded the trumpet blast, Joshua commanded the people, "Shout! For the LORD has given you the city! The city and all that is in it are to be devoted to the LORD. Only Rahab the prostitute and all who are with her in her house shall be spared, because she hid the spies we sent. But keep away from the devoted things, so that you will not bring about your own destruction by taking any of them. Otherwise you will make the camp of Israel liable to destruction and bring trouble on it. All the silver and gold and the articles of bronze and iron are sacred to the LORD and must go into his treasury."
>
> When the trumpets sounded, the people shouted, and at the sound of the trumpet, when the people gave a loud shout, the wall collapsed; so every man charged straight in, and they took the city. (Joshua 6:15-20)

Oriented Leaders understand. Pressing members to move from of the passivity of the wilderness to the manna-free realm of the promised goal requires the long process of discipline.

Discipline: Because Organization isn't Natural

Oriented Leaders understand that the capacity for movement requires sustained energy and relentless organization. The energy for movement does not naturally unfold. The energy to move is cultivated from within and the discipline to harness the energy must come from leadership.

"Without vision, the people perish," goes the proverb (Proverbs 29:18a), and the temptation is to gaze off toward a distant horizon straining our eyes to see things that are not yet present. But the vision of the proverb is not the wistful hope of waiting for things to effortlessly change. The vision of the proverb is a disciplined capacity to move from present reality to attainable possibility.

The full proverb confirms the intimate relationship between discipline and vision.

> "Where there is no vision, the people perish: but *he that keepeth the law, happy is he."* (Proverbs 29:18 KJV) [Italics mine]

Like glasses improve our ability to see what is *actually* there, so too Oriented Leadership clarifies circumstance and organizes plans. Transformative orientation accurately recognizes both the present reality *and* the future possibility. Orientation for a congregation means first seeing what *is,* then charting a course from here to the envisioned future, and finally, moving the people along that course.

Leaders in floundering organizations seldom lack the ability to imagine what "should" be, their struggle lies in an inability to order and discipline the people to move to where they *could* be.

Discipline is the restraint—the "keeping of the law"—which orders the people towards better outcomes.

Joshua learned this hard lesson by watching Moses' mistakes.

After routing the Amalekites in Exodus 18, Moses and the Israelites are camping at Rephidim. Family came from out-of-town. Moses' father-in-law has heard of the great success and decided to check in on his daughter's husband.

Proud of his accomplishments,

> Moses went out to meet his father-in-law and bowed down and kissed him. They greeted each other and then went into the tent. Moses told his father-in-law about everything the LORD had done to Pharaoh and the Egyptians for Israel's sake and about all the hardships they had met along the way and how the LORD had saved them.

Jethro was delighted to hear about all the good things the LORD had done for Israel in rescuing them from the hand of the Egyptians. He said, 'Praise be to the LORD, who rescued you from the hand of the Egyptians and of Pharaoh, and who rescued the people from the hand of the Egyptians. Now I know that the LORD is greater than all other gods, for he did this to those who had treated Israel arrogantly.' (Exodus 18:7-11)

Father-in-law, Jethro, is impressed and celebrates with Moses.

Jethro, brings a burnt offering and other sacrifices to God. Aaron comes with all the elders of Israel to eat bread with Moses' father-in-law in the presence of God. (Exodus 18:12)

Following the celebration, however, Jethro finds reason to doubt the wisdom of his grandchildren's father.

The next day Moses took his seat to serve as judge for the people, and they stood around him from morning till evening. When his father-in-law saw all that Moses was doing for the people, he said, "What is this you are doing for the people? Why do you alone sit as judge, while all these people stand around you from morning till evening?" Moses answered him, "Because the people come to me to seek God's will. Whenever they have a dispute, it is brought to me, and I decide between the parties and inform them of God's decrees and laws."

Moses' father-in-law replied, "What you are doing is not good. You and these people who come to you will only wear yourselves out. The work is too heavy for you; you cannot handle it alone. Listen now to me and I will give you some advice, and may God be with you. You must be the people's representative before God and bring their disputes to him. Teach them the decrees and laws, and show them the way to live and the duties they are to perform. But select capable men from all the people—men who fear

---

God, trustworthy men who hate dishonest gain—and appoint them as officials over thousands, hundreds, fifties and tens. Have them serve as judges for the people at all times, but have them bring every difficult case to you; the simple cases they can decide themselves. That will make your load lighter, because they will share it with you. If you do this and God so commands, you will be able to stand the strain, and all these people will go home satisfied."

Moses listened to his father-in-law and did everything he said. He chose capable men from all Israel and made them leaders of the people, officials over thousands, hundreds, fifties and tens. They served as judges for the people at all times. The difficult cases they brought to Moses, but the simple ones they decided themselves. (Exodus 18:13-26)

Tired of Jethro's meddling,

Moses sent his father-in-law on his way, and Jethro returned to his own country. (Exodus 18:27)

What Jethro proposed was a disciplined administrative process. Administration clarifies the order whereby priority is given to the voice of some individuals and dismisses the voice of others. The documentation of administration includes constitutions, bylaws, procedure manuals, and reports. They assist groups in determining how conflicting "spirits" are weighed or measured they provide guidance for the practice of spiritual gifts, and outline steps towards the implementation of "Spirit-led" decisions.

Jethro's Plan at Raphidim: The first organizational chart

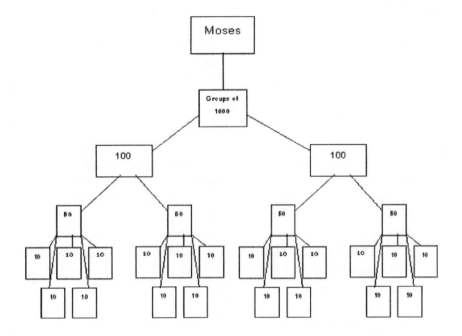

Perhaps the structure was a little too complicated for Moses, perhaps it was difficult for Moses to delegate through an organization that looked like a pyramid. Regardless of the reason, the administration of Jethro's plan fails. Moses documented the creation of judicial councils (Deuteronomy 1:9-18), but there is no evidence he used the dispute-resolution system outlined by Jethro.

We know Moses failed to use the plan because just a few months later he faces exactly the same problem as the people set out from Mount Sinai and arrive at Kibroth Hattaavah.

> Moses heard the people of every family wailing, each at the entrance to his tent. The LORD became exceedingly angry, and Moses was troubled. He asked the LORD, "Why have you brought this trouble on your servant? What have I done to displease you that you put the burden of all these people on me? Did I conceive all these people? Did I give them birth? Why do you tell me to carry them in my arms, as a nurse carries an infant, to the land you promised on oath to their forefathers? Where can I get meat for all these people? They keep wailing to me, 'Give us meat to eat!' I cannot carry all these people by myself; the burden is too heavy for me. If this is how you are going to treat me, put me to death right now—if I have found favor in your eyes—and do not let me face my own ruin."
>
> The LORD said to Moses: "Bring me seventy of Israel's elders who are known to you as leaders and officials among the people. Have them come to the Tent of Meeting, that they may stand there with you. I will come down and speak with you there, and I will take of the Spirit that is on you and put the Spirit on them. They will help you carry the burden of the people so that you will not have to carry it alone." (Numbers 11:10-17)

God's proposal in Numbers 11 is similar to Jethro's solution in Exodus 18. Divide the people into smaller groups and appoint effective leaders over each subgroup, but the second organizational chart is even more streamlined.

Streamlined Council: The second organizational chart

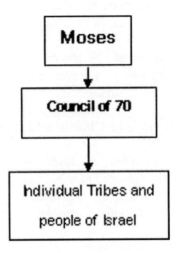

Moses fails to use this organizational structure as well. Throughout the remainder of the Pentateuch, Moses suffers the consequences of micro-management, unreliable reporting, and fickle commitment—in short, the hallmarks of poor discipline. Moses fails as an administrator, not from a lack of planning (Leviticus and Deuteronomy are full of instructions), but from his unwillingness to use an organized administration to resolve conflict. The implication for congregational management is significant. Poor administration will not only scatter the people, in the end it will bring down the leader.

Given two organizational options, one by Jethro the other by God, Moses failed to use either. Throughout the Pentateuch there is absolutely no mention of a dispute, frustration, or disappointment resolved by appointed officials. As a result, Moses was constantly exhausted by the burden of direct responsibility. Every decision, every question, every adjudication had to pass across Moses' desk. He became bewildered by the minutia of operations, he failed to use the gifts and qualifications of those whom he already knew were fit for positions of leadership.

> (The LORD said to Moses: "Bring me seventy of Israel's elders *who are known to you as leaders* and officials among the people." (Numbers 11:16))

Discipline: Because you have to Choose and Use Good People

What I find troubling in ministry are leaders who delegate responsibility to individuals who are poorly equipped to wield that responsibility, sometimes appointing the most undisciplined, disoriented members to positions of authority. As a result, when conflict or complexity arises, the pastor has to step-in to "save" the organization.

In many congregations the individuals given the greatest responsibility are those who are the most manipulative and poorly equipped to lead. These appointed leaders then use their position in the community as extensions of their own wills, calling on the best language of Christian love and charity to bend the organization's agenda towards their own pain relief. People, who we would not allow to borrow our cars, handle our personal finances, or tuck-in our children at night, are handed positions of responsibility to oversee congregational fellowship, supervise church expenditures, and direct educational programs. Consequently, much of what is called congregational ministry tends to flow towards the accommodation of pathology.

As a consultant, I've discovered the 95/5 rule. The 80/20 rule was developed for business, 80% of the work is performed by 20% of the energy. In many congregations, I've found 95% of the pastor's time is spent addressing pathology and only 5% reinforcing health.

One of the greatest mistakes I made at the beginning of my ministry was to devote excessive attention to people with chronic emotional and spiritual sickness. I believed the power of the church could "fix" them, even if they had no desire to be made well. By the time I finished ministering to all the troubled, dysfunctional, and destructive people in the congregation, I had very little energy left to encourage the strong or express gratitude to the competent members of the congregation.

I had foolishly decided the best way to minister to troubled people was to give them responsibility. I actually believed this "higher calling" would encourage their better functioning. If nothing else, by placing them in key positions, I could keep an eye on them so they couldn't do much damage.

At one point my careful work with the nominating committee resulted in no fewer than three of the most confused, troubled, and emotionally immature people in the congregation serving on the board of elders at the same time!

What in God's name was I thinking?

Then, as if to confirm my cluelessness, I spent my time defending these troubled "leaders" from the reasonable expectations of healthy members.

When things didn't get better, I figured I was the problem because these individuals were not becoming healthier, nor was the congregation getting stronger. I internalized the problem deciding that I needed to work harder, preach better, and pray more fervently. During those days, I kept my personal coach very busy.

Healthy relationships in a congregation are not created by an over-functioning pastor. It came to me like a wrestling angel. If a church can't run while the pastor occasionally gets a reasonable night's sleep, then that church worships a very strange God indeed, one who consumes pastors in order to save congregations.

I remembered the words of Fr. James Creighton, a wise chaplain who had supervised my Clinical Pastoral Education a few years before. "The last time I checked," Fr. Jim told me, "the Church believes in only ONE atoning sacrifice, and I have news for you, it is NOT Jonathan Krogh!"

By focusing on the pathology and allowing emotionally unhealthy people to take positions of responsibility, it was as if I said to an infection, "Here are all the resources of the organism available at your disposal. Use them as you wish."

Pathology only knows how to grow pathology. Undisciplined people do not become better disciplined when handed more responsibility, and no amount of insight, resources, or time will change the outcome.

Unfortunately for the congregation, I confused the ministry to empower the oppressed with the activity of accommodating dysfunction.[8]

---

[8] In a theological sense I had misunderstood Jesus' ministry to the lame, the forgotten, and the oppressed. Jesus cared for them not because they were on the bottom; he cared for them because they were the most emotionally healthy members of his society. The outcasts and sinners were the ones who could bring transformation because they functioned without blaming or shaming those around them. It was not their social position that drew Jesus' attention; it was their spiritual and emotional health. Jesus' ministry was not to accommodate their weakness, but to highlight and empower their strength. As Jesus often declared, "*Your* faith has made you well!"

I also recalled Peter Steinke's words at a conference, "There is a fundamental difference between being a fool for Christ and being a damn fool."

Two issues blurred my vision; they are recurring distractions for many congregations.

First, we live in a chronically anxious society which demands "quick-fixes" from its institutions—especially those institutions which articulate values. In light of this anxiety churches are pressured to become ridged rather than relational. This anxiety screams for the elimination of ambiguity and paradox. Like frightened children, the most dysfunctional individuals in our culture beg for us to make decisions on their behalf.

Candidating pastors are no longer asked for statements of faith, instead they are asked litmus questions on issues. Not, "How do you believe God's Spirit is discerned in a congregation?" but, "What is your conclusion about a particular set of cultural questions?" Leadership, which should constantly observe, connect, and reform, has come to mean "certainty" regarding a ridged set of conclusions.

I accommodated the most anxious inquisitors in my congregation by giving them positions of power. Enamored with their authority they ceased to challenge my opinions. Now, because they were the leaders, their anxiety infected the whole congregation.

Second, denominations are becoming increasingly fearful of decline, claiming their congregations have become irrelevant to the realities of modern life. (It is predicted that by the year 2040, my own denomination, the PC (USA) will have a negative 3,200 members.)

What strikes me as odd is how the strongest accusations of the church's irrelevance arise from those for whom the church should be most relevant—the clergy. It causes me to ask, "If the church is so irrelevant, then why did you become a pastor?" Either you are unlike other people because you have found this irrelevant church to be compelling, or you are completely irrational.

I believe congregations become relevant to people's lives insofar as they model and honor spiritual and emotional health.

Healthy communities of faith have never been about *solving* people's problems. They have been about empowering healthy people to solve their own problems. "*Your* faith has made you well!" said Jesus (Luke 17:19). In order for vision to take hold, it is vital for congregations to express and model clear definitions not only of faith, but also of wellness.

Unfortunately, cultural anxiety keeps pushing for rapid relief. For example, there was a time when the educational degrees associated with ministry were primarily from the humanities: art, literature, music, philosophy, foreign languages. Now the primary joint-degree programs are in helping professions: social services, public policy, gerontology, psychology, education, and marketing.

No longer are congregations asking their professional leaders to draw from the "humane", instead they are asking for professionals to provide the technical capacity to "help".

I do not mean to disparage helping disciplines or the usefulness of such joint-degree programs. I only mean to suggest we not buy into the anxious request for the church to "fix" things. We cannot conform to a model of effectiveness which focuses on treating problems rather than reinforcing health.

In my own congregation I accommodated pathology thinking it would increase the relevance of the community to hurting people. But allowing hurting people to assume positions of leadership did not heal their wounds, it gave them the power to hurt others.

Congregations must promote, reward, and empower the spiritually healthy individuals in their midst. I am convinced there is nothing more powerful then how we share our time, our attention, and our resources. How the pastor spends his or her time and energy, models for the congregation what that community finds honorable.

Rabbi Edwin Friedman identified the best leaders in any family, biological or congregational, as those who adapt towards strength rather than weakness.[9]

If we fixate on people who are emotionally dysfunctional, just because they demand our time, then we give our members permission to go home and devote their attention to the most pathological elements of their lives.

When I came to my senses, my vision cleared. I put the congregation and myself on notice; we would no longer abdicate the community's agenda by compromising with complainers. Such compromise had become habitual, and the neediness of a few sapped the creativity, imagination, and love from the life of a congregation. Each compromise I had justified with the promise that "this is the *last* time", only to be manipulated again into submission at the next cry for help. If my ministry was going to be effective, there really had to be a *last time*.

I proposed a new tact for the nominating committee, suggesting we nominate only our top choice for every position. The nominating committee was asked to fill positions of leadership with the most emotionally healthy people they knew, even if they had never served in a leadership position before. If an individual seemed to come from the "B-list", that person would not be nominated, even if the position remained unfilled. As a result the nominating committee presented

---

9   Edwin H. Friedman, *A Failure of Nerve: Leadership in the Age of the Quick Fix* (New York: Seabury Books, 2007) 231.

some incomplete slates to the congregation, some positions remained unfilled. But even with smaller committees and boards, we became more effective.

When I moved towards reinforcing health rather than pathology, three interesting things happened. First, within six months, the most dysfunctional members of the board resigned or decided not to stand for reelection. Second, gifted, thoughtful people who had decreased their involvement were now asking to be trained for leadership. Third, I found myself enjoying pastoral ministry again.

Discipline: Because the Wrong People will Take Charge

Joshua witnessed Moses actively undermine Jethro's and God's organizational charts. When the people complained for lack of water, food, or meat, they whined to Moses hoping to change their plight. Again and again, rather than being decisive, Moses complained to God. Never truly owning his call, Moses perpetually deflected responsibility.

God tried to help. Inherited-Tradition endowed Moses with the power of Divine blessing. Moses would have to lead the people alone unless God transferred some authority to others, which is exactly what happened in front of the Tent of Meeting in Numbers 11.

Through a selection process, seventy were specifically chosen to share leadership with Moses. We are given no detail regarding the selection process, but we do know Moses was to set aside those who demonstrated good leadership skills.

> "Bring me seventy of Israel's elders" commanded God,
> "Who are known to you as leaders and officials among
> the people." (Numbers 11:16a)

The stage was set for a crucial moment in the formation of the nation, the possibility of intergenerational succession. If handled correctly, authority would no longer depend on a burning bush or favored bloodline; Moses could delegate and finally relax. A fixed council of seventy would be selected based on criteria of competence, and members could be replaced as necessary. The progression from Traditional to Rational-Legal Authority would secure identity and continuity, but Moses blew it.

No doubt succession was on Joshua's mind. Already identified as the heir apparent to Moses' authority, Joshua knew an orderly transfer of power would help him in the future to gain the nation's allegiance. If the children of Israel witnessed Moses publically delegating his Traditional Authority through a Rational-Legal process, Joshua's ascendancy to command would be easier.

> Then the LORD came down in the cloud and spoke with [Moses], and he took of the Spirit that was on him and put the Spirit on the seventy elders. When the Spirit rested on them, they prophesied, but they did not do so again. (Numbers 11:25)

The confirmation of the transfer of power was the prophetic utterances of the newly installed council. These prophesies immediately followed the inauguration, giving charismatic confirmation of the selection process. (Not unlike the first 100 days of a newly installed congress, during which the nation watches to see if wise action confirms the accuracy of election.) As the prophetic Spirit rested on the members of the council, the watching public was assured that the selection process was correct. They had identified the best leaders for the job.

But, as the text points out, they never prophesied again. Why? Because Moses had undermined the process!

> However, two men, whose names were Eldad and Medad, had remained in the camp. They were listed among the elders, but did not go out to the Tent. Yet the Spirit also rested on them, and they prophesied in the camp. A young man ran and told Moses, "Eldad and Medad are prophesying in the camp."

> Joshua son of Nun, who had been Moses' aide since youth, spoke up and said, "Moses, my lord, stop them!"

> But Moses replied, "Are you jealous for my sake? I wish that all the LORD's people were prophets and that the LORD would put his Spirit on them!" Then Moses and the elders of Israel returned to the camp. (Numbers 11:26-30)

Two charismatic yahoos, Eldad and Medad, decided to self-appoint. They hadn't completed a resume, they failed to attend the training, and until that moment they were of no consequence to formation of the nation. Without right or justification they began to function as if they were members of the leadership council.

Allowing Eldad and Medad to prophesy, Moses permitted interlopers to attach publicly to the legitimately installed leadership, even though their right to power was not through legal means. Spontaneous charismatic participation was their only claim to the rights of leadership. No wonder Joshua was furious.

Moses' action illustrates how quickly leaders can sabotage effectiveness. In rejecting Joshua's advice Moses immediately invalidated the legitimacy of the council. If anyone with a charismatic experience was validated for leadership, then the process of examination and selection is rendered pointless.

> **Moses proclaims, "Are you jealous for my sake? I wish that all the LORD's people were prophets and that the LORD would put his Spirit on them." (Numbers 11:29)**

As a consequence, the council becomes an unqualified failure. Three things happened: 1) this is the last time Joshua offers any advice to Moses, 2) the council never again utters prophecy, and 3) there is no record of the seventy participating in any leadership decisions.

From that moment on, even God's strategy changed. Moses received no further assistance in power sharing.

Discipline: The Responsibility of Leadership

Moses took the job of leader personally. He suggests Joshua is protesting because of his jealousy of Moses rather than Joshua's jealousy for the people.

When dealing with disciplined power-sharing the leader's ego can get in the way. As a consultant I have witnessed emerging leadership rendered powerless by the "old guard's" tendency to take change personally. A beloved tradition, program, or structure is defended not on the grounds of institutional need or organizational effectiveness, but because new leaders are told not to hurt the former leaders' feelings.

Joshua's protest of Eldad and Medad was not because he feared for Moses, but because Joshua feared for the people. Joshua knew if they were to become a nation, they had to imagine their life beyond Moses. In brittle moments of transition, the people needed Moses to use his power to share his authority. Joshua was asking Moses to make a decisive choice to defend the process by being jealous for the legitimacy of the council. Seeing the advice as a personal attack, Moses lost an important step in disciplined organization building.

Moses even blames God for needing a leadership council in the first place. Moses suggests the people are complaining because God hasn't made them more "spiritual". If God would just give them the appropriate gifts and make them all men of prophesy, Moses wouldn't need to hear their complaints and they wouldn't need a council. If the people would simply do the right thing in the first place, they wouldn't be such a burden on his leadership.

To blame a congregation's lack of vision on the shallow spirituality of the people, is to wait for health and vitality to fall from the heaven like so much *manna*—imagining that the only hope for revival arises from God's mysterious hand touching each and every human heart.

I've witnessed committee meetings completely wasted as leaders lament the need for decisiveness. "If only people could do what they are supposed to do," goes the complaint. And then the next several hours of valuable time is wasted while the leaders wring their hands over the inadequacy of the rank and file. While it may be true that leadership exists because people are fallible, it is a waste of time to long for the community of the perfect.

Discipline: Because People *Kvetch*

Such complaints remind me of librarians who claim their work would be easier if people quit un-shelving books, or maintenance personnel who complain that people keep getting things dirty. Leaders are necessary because people clamor, confuse, and kvetch.

The true hallmark of wilderness living was not the redemption of a people, the business of nation building, or the promise of conquest. The hallmark of wilderness life was the complaining by the people. A rabbinic colleague of mine identified these days in the Bible as "Forty Years of Kvetching."

I find this wonderful Yiddish term helpful because I find the term descriptive of the behavior of most religious communities.

From Webster's: **kvetch** (kvĕch) *Slang intr.v.* **kvetched, kvetch·ing, kvetch·es**
To complain persistently and whiningly.
noun.

1. A chronic, whining complainer.
2. A nagging complaint: "a rambling kvetch against the system" (Leonard Ross).
   [From the Yiddish kvetshn, *to squeeze, complain*, **from Middle High German** quetzen, quetschen, *to squeeze*.**]**

Congregational leaders should find comfort in this reality, recorded as the first collective response of God's chosen people. When they spoke with one voice it was usually to murmur and complain. It is helpful in the midst of any congregational meeting, administrative council, or denominational gathering to remember that the most enduring identity of God's chosen people was "kvetchers".

- ❧ Exodus 5:21-23 Bricks without straw—the people kvetch
- ❧ Exodus 14:10-12 Egyptians in pursuit—the people kvetch
- ❧ Exodus 15:22-16:3 No bread or meat—the people kvetch
- ❧ Exodus 17:1-3 No water to drink—the people kvetch

When faced with shortages and hard times, the overriding response of the people was complaint. Their complaints were damaging because Moses failed to maintain a systematic structure for grievance.

Not that there are fewer complaints when there is an effective organizational structure, it is simply that without a disciplined means of communication and enforcement, complaints are all the community hears.

Frustration that dissention is "getting in the way" of ministry is to misunderstand the leader's call. Ministry includes many facets, but one of them MUST be creating disciplined systems for addressing dissention. Organizing and maintaining a system of dispute resolution is not an intrusion into leadership, it is one of the jobs of leadership. When structures of accountability fail, kvetching is all the leaders will experience, and the other more interesting leadership duties (envisioning, creating, and moving) become impossible.

Disciplined: Because Crisis Intervention is Too Much Work

Throughout Joshua's life, discipline was his passion. Whether commanding the Israelite army to their first victory over the Amalekites (Exodus 17), or recognizing the possible warfare among the people who had built a calf-god (Exodus 32), or attempting to silence Eldad and Medad in the desert of Paran (Numbers 11), or participating with Caleb in the minority spy report (Numbers 13 and 14), Joshua never forgot his purpose or direction. He continually understood that the people had left Egypt in order to enter the Promised Land.

Unfortunately, even the long marches around Jericho were not enough. The people were still not sufficiently disciplined to be an army.

At Jericho, Joshua commanded the people to take no plunder. Commanding them to keep their hands off the devoted things required discipline.

From his orientation for the long-haul, Joshua understood the spoils of Jericho would finance upcoming military campaigns. In the wilderness, precious metals for trade and hardened metals for war were scarce. The gold and silver they had brought from Egypt had already been used for the construction of the

Ark of the Covenant and the Tabernacle (Exodus 25:1-7), or had been ground into powder as punishment for the Golden Calf, (Exodus 32:20). If Joshua was going to wage war from the Jordan crossing to the shoreline of Mahalab (Joshua 19:29), the treasury was going to need every resource from the sacking of Jericho. Sadly, not everyone believed Joshua was serious. Akin took a souvenir.

Fresh from the victory at Jericho the army believed they were invincible. But they had won through no strategy or strength of their own. Unfortunately, human nature breeds a hubris that sees failure as someone else's fault and victory as self-affirmation.

Joshua's spies were sent to Ai.

> When they returned to Joshua, they said, "Not all the people will have to go up against Ai. Send two or three thousand men to take it and do not weary all the people, for only a few men are there." So about three thousand men went up; but they were routed by the men of Ai, who killed about thirty-six of them. They chased the Israelites from the city gate as far as the stone quarries and struck them down on the slopes. At this the hearts of the people melted and became like water.

> Then Joshua tore his clothes and fell facedown to the ground before the ark of the LORD, remaining there till evening. The elders of Israel did the same and sprinkled dust on their heads. And Joshua said, "Ah, Sovereign LORD, why did you ever bring this people across the Jordan to deliver us into the hands of the Amorites to destroy us? If only we had been content to stay on the other side of the Jordan! O Lord, what can I say, now that Israel has been routed by its enemies? The Canaanites and the other people of the country will hear about this and they will surround us and wipe out our name from the earth. What then will you do for your own great name?"

> The LORD said to Joshua, "Stand up! What are you doing down on your face? Israel has sinned; they have violated my covenant, which I commanded them to keep. They have taken some of the devoted things; they have stolen, they have lied, they have put them with their own possessions. That is why the Israelites cannot

stand against their enemies; they turn their backs and run because they have been made liable to destruction. I will not be with you anymore unless you destroy whatever among you is devoted to destruction.

"Go, consecrate the people. Tell them, 'Consecrate yourselves in preparation for tomorrow; for this is what the LORD, the God of Israel, says: That which is devoted is among you, O Israel. You cannot stand against your enemies until you remove it.

"'In the morning, present yourselves tribe by tribe. The tribe that the LORD takes shall come forward clan by clan; the clan that the LORD takes shall come forward family by family; and the family that the LORD takes shall come forward man by man. He who is caught with the devoted things shall be destroyed by fire, along with all that belongs to him. He has violated the covenant of the LORD and has done a disgraceful thing in Israel!'"

Early the next morning Joshua had Israel come forward by tribes, and Judah was taken. The clans of Judah came forward, and he took the Zerahites. He had the clan of the Zerahites come forward by families, and Zimri was taken. Joshua had his family come forward man by man, and Achan son of Carmi, the son of Zimri, the son of Zerah, of the tribe of Judah, was taken.

Then Joshua said to Achan, "My son, give glory to the LORD, the God of Israel, and give him the praise. Tell me what you have done; do not hide it from me."

Achan replied, "It is true! I have sinned against the LORD, the God of Israel. This is what I have done: When I saw in the plunder a beautiful robe from Babylonia, two hundred shekels of silver and a wedge of gold weighing fifty shekels, I coveted them and took them. They are hidden in the ground inside my tent, with the silver underneath."

So Joshua sent messengers, and they ran to the tent, and there it was, hidden in his tent, with the silver underneath. They took the things from the tent, brought them to Joshua and all the Israelites and spread them out before the LORD.

Then Joshua, together with all Israel, took Achan son of Zerah, the silver, the robe, the gold wedge, his sons and daughters, his cattle, donkeys and sheep, his tent and all that he had, to the Valley of Achor. Joshua said, "Why have you brought this trouble on us? The LORD will bring trouble on you today."

Then all Israel stoned him, and after they had stoned the rest, they burned them. Over Achan they heaped up a large pile of rocks, which remains to this day. Then the LORD turned from his fierce anger. Therefore that place has been called the Valley of Achor ever since. (Joshua 7:3-26)

At Ai Joshua responds with five steps for problem solving, not crisis intervention.

1. Joshua identified the problem. Devoted objects were taken from Jericho.
2. He announces the sentence prior to finding the culprit. The one who took the objects will be destroyed together with everything they own.
3. He investigates to discover who was at fault, tribe by tribe, clan by clan, family by family, and man by man.
4. He follows through with the punishment. Achan son of Zerah is stoned with all he owns and then burned.
5. He returns to the business of conquering the Promised Land (Joshua 8), this time with the entire army.

Joshua's response to the defeat at Ai stands in significant contrast to Moses' response to the Golden Calf. Both events occur after significant military victory (the Golden Calf after the defeat of the Amalekites (Exodus 17) and the defeat at Ai after the victory over Jericho (Joshua 6)). It may be due to false confidence, pride, or stupidity, but whatever the reason it is axiomatic, rebellion follows success.

Joshua's response to the rebellion was not rage. There is no smashing of tablets, no slaughter of 3,000, no bitter medicine. For a brief moment Joshua takes a page from Moses' leadership manual and broods (Joshua 7:6-9). But because Joshua understands his Oriented Authority, God wastes little time in commanding Joshua to "QUIT IT!" (Joshua 7:10). Joshua was personally disciplined enough to enforce group discipline and move forward.

Disciplined leaders do not see setbacks as crises, they see them as one more opportunity to solve problems and move forward.

CHAPTER VI

Evidence of Oriented Leadership—Integrity

T he final test of Oriented Leadership is *integrity,* particularly in the face of failure.

Months after his encounter with the commander of the army of the LORD, Joshua's integrity was put the test when he was duped by the Gibeonites.

> Now when all the kings west of the Jordan heard about [the destruction of Jericho and Ai]—those in the hill country, in the western foothills, and along the entire coast of the Great Sea as far as Lebanon (the kings of the Hittites, Amorites, Canaanites, Perizzites, Hivites and Jebusites)—they came together to make war against Joshua and Israel.
>
> However, when the people of Gibeon heard what Joshua had done to Jericho and Ai, they resorted to a ruse: They went as a delegation whose donkeys were loaded with worn-out sacks and old wineskins, cracked and mended. The men put worn and patched sandals on their feet and wore old clothes. All the bread of their food supply was dry and moldy. Then they went to Joshua in the camp at Gilgal and said to him and the men of Israel, "We have come from a distant country; make a treaty with us."

The men of Israel said to the Hivites, "But perhaps you live near us. How then can we make a treaty with you?"

"We are your servants," they said to Joshua.
But Joshua asked, "Who are you and where do you come from?"

They answered: "Your servants have come from a very distant country because of the fame of the LORD your God. For we have heard reports of him: all that he did in Egypt, and all that he did to the two kings of the Amorites east of the Jordan—Sihon king of Heshbon, and Og king of Bashan, who reigned in Ashtaroth. And our elders and all those living in our country said to us, 'Take provisions for your journey; go and meet them and say to them, "We are your servants; make a treaty with us." 'This bread of ours was warm when we packed it at home on the day we left to come to you. But now see how dry and moldy it is. And these wineskins that we filled were new, but see how cracked they are. And our clothes and sandals are worn out by the very long journey.'

The men of Israel sampled their provisions but did not inquire of the LORD. Then Joshua made a treaty of peace with them to let them live, and the leaders of the assembly ratified it by oath.

Three days after they made the treaty with the Gibeonites, the Israelites heard that they were neighbors, living near them. So the Israelites set out and on the third day came to their cities: Gibeon, Kephirah, Beeroth and Kiriath Jearim. But the Israelites did not attack them, because the leaders of the assembly had sworn an oath to them by the LORD, the God of Israel.

The whole assembly grumbled against the leaders, but all the leaders answered, "We have given them our oath by the LORD, the God of Israel, and we cannot touch them now. This is what we will do to them: We will let them live, so that wrath will not fall on us for breaking the oath we swore to them." They continued, "Let them live, but let them be woodcutters and water carriers for the entire community." So the leaders' promise to them was kept.

Then Joshua summoned the Gibeonites and said, "Why did you deceive us by saying, 'we live a long way from you,' while actually you live near us? You are now under a curse: You will never cease to serve as woodcutters and water carriers for the house of my God."

They answered Joshua, "Your servants were clearly told how the LORD your God had commanded his servant Moses to give you the whole land and to wipe out all its inhabitants from before you. So we feared for our lives because of you, and that is why we did this. We are now in your hands. Do to us whatever seems good and right to you."

So Joshua saved them from the Israelites, and they did not kill them. That day he made the Gibeonites woodcutters and water carriers for the community and for the altar of the LORD at the place the LORD would choose. And that is what they are to this day. (Joshua chapter 9)

Not long after the treaty, Joshua made good on his promise to protect the Gibeonites.

Now Adoni-Zedek, king of Jerusalem, heard that Joshua had taken Ai and totally destroyed it, doing to Ai and its king as he had done to Jericho and its king; and that the people of Gibeon had made a treaty of peace with Israel and were living near them. He and his people were very much alarmed at this, because Gibeon was an important city, like one of the royal cities; it was larger than Ai, and all its men were good fighters. So Adoni-Zedek king of Jerusalem appealed to Hoham king of Hebron, Piram king of Jarmuth, Japhia king of

Lachish and Debir king of Eglon, "Come up and help me attack Gibeon," he said, "because it has made peace with Joshua and the Israelites."

Then the five kings of the Amorites—the kings of Jerusalem, Hebron, Jarmuth, Lachish and Eglon—joined forces. They moved up with all their troops and took up positions against Gibeon and attacked it.

The Gibeonites then sent word to Joshua in the camp at Gilgal: "Do not abandon your servants. Come up to us quickly and save us! Help us, because all the Amorite kings from the hill country have joined forces against us."

So Joshua marched up from Gilgal with his entire army, including all the best fighting men. The LORD said to Joshua, "Do not be afraid of them; I have given them into your hand. Not one of them will be able to withstand you."

After an all-night march from Gilgal, Joshua took them by surprise. The LORD threw them into confusion before Israel, who defeated them in a great victory at Gibeon. (Joshua 10:1-10)

In light of the Gibeonite deception Joshua could have justified their slaughter at the hand of Adnoi-zedek. He could have appealed to the goal of total conquest. After all, the Gibeonite's blood would be on the hands of Adnoi-zedek not Joshua. But Joshua's integrity was even greater than his desire for conquest.

Allowing the Gibeonites to survive was inconvenient, especially since their survival was based on a deception, but for years to come, the Israelites would accommodate the Gibeonites who lived in a protected sanctuary just south of Ai. Generations later, King David was bound to protect them because of Joshua's oath (II Samuel 21).

Oriented Leadership seeks no simple solution. Joshua chose to do what was inconvenient. He protected the Gibeonites because he was committed to integrity, not expedience.

Orientated Leadership requires courage. Not a swashbuckling disregard for safety that stands against impossible odds, but the humble courage to look beyond simple solutions to the very character of an organization. Oriented

Leadership pushes relentlessly for coherence, focus, clear reporting, and fairness. Underlying each of these dimensions is a single purpose—integrity.

Oriented Leadership: An Environment for Integrity to Flourish

Integrity has come to mean honesty, but the word means so much more. Integrity goes beyond the moral decisions of individuals to include the quality of relationships between individuals and the structural connection of the entire organization. Because integrity is at the core of ethical behavior, Oriented Leaders seek to organize the system so that accountability reinforces honesty.

An ethical environment allows individuals to balance moral choices in their decision making. Unethical behavior is not created by a few "bad apples", it is abetted by environments which fail to provide the necessary checks of discipline and balances of rewards. A system of integrity reveals unethical behavior and moral compromise stands out as an aberration. As a result, unethical options are less likely to be considered in the first place.

A system of integrity allows each part to carry the load in proportion to its strength. Consider of the construction of a bridge. A bridge constructed with integrity allows each beam, column, piling, and rivet to carry its load in an engineered complement, so that stress placed on the bridge as a *whole* does not overwhelm any *part*.

When bridges or organizations fail, the temptation is to blame the part that "broke". But more often than not, failure is the result of poor design or neglected maintenance. The buckling and twisting which causes a given piece to snap is usually not the result of the piece's weakness, but the result of a design which placed undue stress on that single component.

Similarly the pressure for moral compromise in an organization frequently comes from unreasonable amount of pressure placed on particular individuals who are compensating for the underperformance of others.

This is not to say that well-integrated systems will consistently prevent individuals from making unethical decisions. There will always be those who circumvent accountability for personal gain. Nor do systems which lack integrity excuse those who make unethical choices; personal accountability can never be waved. It simply means that the likelihood for individuals to struggle with the pressures of moral ambiguity increases when the organization lacks integrity.

Like the toddler who "acts out" when his parents fight, the disruptive members of a congregational family exhibit their weakness when the system fails to ensure the accountability of its leaders.

One of my client congregations appeared to be split over the ordination of women. The anxiety ran high as they considered calling a new pastor. As part of the consulting process I interviewed several members and found many who were open to female ordination, but when asked if the congregation would consider the best pastor regardless of gender, they consistently remarked, "I don't think the congregation is ready." For years the issue was avoided in any public forum because most of the members believed it would split the church.

A day arrived, however, when the issue of female ordination was put to the test as the congregation was rewriting its constitution. What was believed to be an even split turned out to be the concern of only three members. The congregation amended their constitution to include the possibility of a female pastor. The crisis, which had threatened to tear the church apart, disappeared when the full membership bore the weight of a vote.

As engineers examine the parts and relationships within a constructed system, so too leaders must carefully examine their congregations to determine if there is a disproportionate distribution of weight given to the attitudes or influences of a few.

Integrity: Removes the Idolatry of the Status Quo

When little children make too much noise for the adults to participate in worship, they are often told, "This is God's House! You need to be more respectful." When we place our gifts in the offering plate we are told, "We are giving our money to God." When we meet a member of the clergy, we are often informed, "He (or she) is ordained by God to do God's work." As we meet for committee meetings, the opening prayer informs us, "We are deciding God's business." When we gather for worship, fellowship, or Christian education, we call ourselves "the Church," and this simply isn't true.

As is the case with many lies, the intentions are good. The lie is told so we will take our corporate religious life more seriously; but as is the case with all lies, regardless of their intent, they are destructive.

The fact is, religious institutions are not sacred—they are merely institutions; and integrity is easier when leaders recognize the human fallibility of their organizations.

For those who pursue ministerial occupations, believing in the "holiness" of the institutional church is especially dangerous. When the organization proves to be all-too-human, illusions become disillusions; and disillusions create burnout. Behaving as if the community and its institutional surroundings are sacred makes an idol of a human structure.

What's more, as the falsehood reveals itself, it is tempting for religious leaders to hold to the lie even more aggressively. In an attempt to explain why a religious institution has behaved in such a human fashion, defenders of the structure claim it is because some have not believed the lie strongly enough. These individuals are then blamed for the institution's fallibility.

Yet the reality remains, institutional congregations are not The Church. The continuing imperfection of human organizations means we can only, at our best, illuminate the truth. Our congregations, denominations, seminaries, and associated religious institutions are NOT manifestations of God's perfect presence, they are simply human organizations incorporated for a specific purpose. They are capable of the same range of greatness and mediocrity expressed in every other human institution.

Congregations are nothing more and nothing less than 501-c3 corporations. If the earthen vessel is mistaken for the treasure, then what unfolds is an idolatry of the container rather than holy respect for its contents.

Congregations and denominational judicatories have historically hidden corruption when their leaders believe their credibility would be lost if the world discovered their fallibility. Oriented Leaders know the danger of such thinking; corruptibility is a given. Because institutions are human, a relentless drive for integrity is the only lasting protection for legitimate authority.

Joshua faced such a concern following the completion of the conquest. The Reubenites, Gadites, and the half-tribe of Manasseh returned west across the Jordan to the homes they had been promised at the beginning of the book. There they constructed their own altar, which the remainder of the nation saw as a declaration of succession.

So the Reubenites, the Gadites and the half-tribe of Manasseh left the Israelites at Shiloh in Canaan to return to Gilead, their own land, which they had acquired in accordance with the command of the LORD through Moses.

When they came to Geliloth near the Jordan in the land of Canaan, the Reubenites, the Gadites and the half-tribe of Manasseh built an imposing altar there by the Jordan. And when the Israelites heard that they had built the altar on the border of Canaan at Geliloth near the Jordan on the Israelite side, the whole assembly of Israel gathered at Shiloh to go to war against them.

So the Israelites sent Phinehas son of Eleazar, the priest, to the land of Gilead—to Reuben, Gad and the half-tribe of Manasseh. With him they sent ten of the chief men, one for each of the tribes of Israel, each the head of a family division among the Israelite clans.

When they went to Gilead—to Reuben, Gad and the half-tribe of Manasseh—they said to them: "The whole assembly of the LORD says: 'How could you break faith with the God of Israel like this? How could you turn away from the LORD and build yourselves an altar in rebellion against him now? Was not the sin of Peor enough for us? Up to this very day we have not cleansed ourselves from that sin, even though a plague fell on the community of the LORD! And are you now turning away from the LORD?

"'If you rebel against the LORD today, tomorrow he will be angry with the whole community of Israel. If the land you possess is defiled, come over to the LORD's land, where the LORD's tabernacle stands, and share the land with us. But do not rebel against the LORD or against us by building an altar for yourselves, other than the altar of the LORD our God. When Achan son of Zerah acted unfaithfully regarding the devoted things, did not wrath come upon the whole community of Israel? He was not the only one who died for his sin.'"

Then Reuben, Gad and the half-tribe of Manasseh replied to the heads of the clans of Israel: "The Mighty One, God, the LORD! The Mighty One, God, the LORD! He knows! And let Israel know! If this has been in rebellion or disobedience to the LORD, do not spare us this day. If we have built our own altar to turn away from the LORD and to offer burnt offerings and grain offerings, or to sacrifice fellowship offerings on it, may the LORD himself call us to account.

"No! We did it for fear that some day your descendants might say to ours, 'What do you have to do with the LORD, the God of Israel? The LORD has made the Jordan a boundary between us and you—you Reubenites and Gadites! You have no share in the LORD.' So your descendants might cause ours to stop fearing the LORD.

—

"That is why we said, 'Let us get ready and build an altar—but not for burnt offerings or sacrifices.' On the contrary, it is to be a witness between us and you and the generations that follow, that we will worship the LORD at his sanctuary with our burnt offerings, sacrifices and fellowship offerings. Then in the future your descendants will not be able to say to ours, 'You have no share in the LORD.'

"And we said, 'If they ever say this to us, or to our descendants, we will answer: Look at the replica of the LORD's altar, which our fathers built, not for burnt offerings and sacrifices, but as a witness between us and you.'

"Far be it from us to rebel against the LORD and turn away from him today by building an altar for burnt offerings, grain offerings and sacrifices, other than the altar of the LORD our God that stands before his tabernacle."

When Phinehas the priest and the leaders of the community—the heads of the clans of the Israelites—heard what Reuben, Gad and Manasseh had to say, they were pleased. And Phinehas son of Eleazar, the priest, said to Reuben, Gad and Manasseh, "Today we know that the LORD is with us, because you have not acted unfaithfully toward the LORD in this matter. Now you have rescued the Israelites from the LORD's hand."

Then Phinehas son of Eleazar, the priest, and the leaders returned to Canaan from their meeting with the Reubenites and Gadites in Gilead and reported to the Israelites. They were glad to hear the report and praised God. And they talked no more about going to war against them to devastate the country where the Reubenites and the Gadites lived.

And the Reubenites and the Gadites gave the altar this name: "A Witness between Us that the LORD is God." (Joshua 22:9-34)

—

Joshua's trusted investigators returned with a favorable report. The altar at Geliloth was the opposite of a declaration of independence; it was a symbol of allegiance. Had Joshua believed the initial report, he would have arrived with a fighting force to coerce compliance, or even worse, assumed the two and one-half tribes were rebels. Instead, Joshua conducted an investigation through a trusted delegation.

Integrity requires time. Joshua could have quickly eliminated the presumed rebellion. Instead, Joshua took the time for a painstaking inspection of circumstance and motive. Too often leaders perceive the work of investigation to be a waste of time. It is much easier to believe the worst and declare war on the opposition in the name of strength. But Oriented Leaders understand how the work for coherence demonstrates a commitment to strength.

Many congregational conflicts arise from presumptions regarding motives. Groups square-off over who "loves their church more", or "understands things better". Diversity of human expression will result in conflict, even when individuals are in agreement. Oriented Leaders do not tolerate rumors; they work for clarity and consistency. Had the tribes east of the Jordan been seeking schism, Joshua no doubt would have enforced their allegiance. But aggressive intervention was unnecessary because Joshua was willing to ask questions and test allegiance rather than presume division.

Integrity: Regularly Tests the System

Simple tests for integrity examine how various areas of an organization respond to stress.

In Chapter Two, I outlined the three forms of organizational structure: Rational-Legal, Inherited-Tradition, and Charismatic-Personality. Disintegration of an organization will manifest itself differently in each of these organizational forms.

The following table outlines the stress response for each of these three authority structures. These tests allow leaders to anticipate the locations of difficulty, and identifies where the most careful inspection should be conducted. While each organizational system "fails" in its own way, the response of Oriented Leadership remains consistent regardless of the organizational form.

Organizational Area	Rational Legal Authority	Inherited Tradition Authority	Charismatic Personality Authority	Oriented Leaders
Decision making	Appeals to "qualifications" of experts	Appeals to precedent and the rights of office	Appeals to the group's "happiness"	Appeal to values & mission
Information Flow	"Need to know" basis	Top down	Leader's prerogative	Accountable process
Policies & Procedures	Excessively detailed & impersonal	Unreflective & poorly articulated	Deemed unnecessary	Clear & appealable
Reorganization	Continual & crisis driven	Unquestioning & autocratic	Whim driven	Preemptive
Documentation	Rigid & petty	"As needed"	Inconsistent & incomplete	Consistent & accurate
Blame	No one is accountable	Idealists or outsiders blamed	Unbelieving insiders blamed	Solutions explored
Creativity	Unfocused & unheard	Pointless & distrusted	Stifled as unnecessary	Problem solving rewarded
Opposition	Quieted by procedural manipulation	To be ignored or destroyed	Untolerated & exiled	Encouraged & accountable
Discipline	Bureaucratic & ineffectual	Swift & unyielding	Personal & public	Private & consistent

Oriented Authority seeks integrity in every dimension of an organization's functioning. Like Joshua protecting the Gibeonites or investigating the altar at Geliloth, transcendent values guide decisions regardless of precedent, competence, or expedience. Information is shared through accountable processes, policies are clear, reorganization is preemptive, and documentation is consistent.

In systems with low integrity, blame becomes more important than solutions. "Who screwed up?" is the operative question, and "How do we fix it?" is seldom addressed. As a result, creativity disappears because individuals are unwilling to risk being wrong. Opposition becomes an irritant to leaders rather than an opportunity for innovation. Organizations without integrity force individuals to fear punishment and humiliation, rather than participate in the shared responsibility of mutual strength.

The twin sins of micromanagement and ignorance run rampant when Oriented Leadership is absent. In an attempt to maintain power, disoriented leaders either inflict their will on the people, or passively wait to join the group's direction.

Tensions between those who wish to solve problems and those who wish to keep the peace weaken the possibility for a congregation's future, so in the wilderness they remain.

Integrity: Because the Stakes are High

Looking back to Joshua's first speech to the people we see his early passion for integrity. Moses had selected Joshua as one of the twelve spies to investigate the Promised Land in preparation for their invasion (Numbers13:8).

Despite Joshua and Caleb's best efforts, they could not overcome a leadership unwilling to challenge the congregation—to seek the integrity of their full identity as the people of God's Promise.

> [The spies] came back to Moses and Aaron and the whole Israelite community at Kadesh in the Desert of Paran. There they reported to them and to the whole assembly and showed them the fruit of the land. They gave Moses this account: "We went into the land to which you sent us, and it does flow with milk and honey! Here is its fruit. But the people who live there are powerful, and the cities are fortified and very large. We even saw descendants of Anak there. The Amalekites live in the Negev; the Hittites, Jebusites and Amorites live in the hill country; and the Canaanites live near the sea and along the Jordan."

> Then Caleb silenced the people before Moses and said,
> "We should go up and take possession of the land, for
> we can certainly do it."
>
> But the men who had gone up with him said, "We can't
> attack those people; they are stronger than we are."
> And they spread among the Israelites a bad report
> about the land they had explored. They said, "The land
> we explored devours those living in it. All the people we
> saw there are of great size. We saw the Nephilim there
> (the descendants of Anak come from the Nephilim).
> We seemed like grasshoppers in our own eyes, and we
> looked the same to them." (Numbers 13:26-33)

After forty days, when the spies returned to camp, the majority report predicted disaster. Their careful analysis projected significant losses if they ventured into the Canaanite territory. Their competition was, after all, giants—mythic Nephilim—the antediluvian thugs for whom Noah's flood had been prepared, the leather-necked descendants of Anak who were trained warriors mighty in battle (Numbers 13:26-39).

Yes, the report of the ten confirmed that the rewards for the victors would be great. There were grapes the size of your fist, pomegranates bigger than melons, milk so rich in butterfat it wouldn't pour, and bee-hives so full and frequent that the forests rained honey.

Disregard the plagues which brought Pharaoh's court to its knees, never mind the annihilation of the far more sophisticated Egyptian army, forget the victory over the Amalekites under Moses' staff—the ten ignored the Divine mandate, the Covenant promise to occupy the ancestral lands of their father Abraham. Standing at the brink of wealth after generations of slavery, gazing over the threshold into opulence, they advised Aaron and Moses to abandon the mission. The band of ten "choked".

The report from this overwhelming majority (a whopping 83%) reviewed the competition, highlighted the strength of the opposition, and concluded advancement into these districts would mean Israelite annihilation. And in response to the majority report, Moses and Aaron crumbled! They put on their rumpled sweat suits, slumped on the couch, refused to shave or bathe, and alternated between open weeping and passive sighing (Numbers 14:5).

Seeing the response of these brother-leaders, the people's enthusiasm understandably evaporates. A vacuum of courage at the top created a schism in the ranks. A faction developed in the camp, one that would challenge the unity of the people for the next forty years. This group made plans to return west. They wanted to slink back to Egypt. Perhaps if they apologized for their rebellion, Pharaoh would give them back their old jobs (Numbers 14:1-4).

There was, however, a minority report filed by Caleb and co-signed by Joshua. These two spies considered the same data as the ten but came to a radically different conclusion.

The introduction of the minority report mirrored that of the majority. The land was indeed rich, "flowing with milk and honey". The inhabitants were big and strong, great battle-tested warriors. But the portion of the report recommending "a course of action" was diametrically opposite to the majority report. Caleb and Joshua unequivocally recommended invasion.

Unable to sway Moses or Aaron into any response, Joshua makes his appeal directly to the people.

> "The land we passed through and explored is exceedingly good,"

Bellowed Joshua to the assembly,

> "If the LORD is pleased with us, he will lead us into that land, a land flowing with milk and honey, and will give it to us. Only do not rebel against the LORD. And do not be afraid of the people of the land, because we will swallow them up. Their protection is gone, but the LORD is with us. Do not be afraid of them." (Numbers 14:6-11)

But it was too late. A spirit of defeatism had gripped the leadership. Neither Joshua nor Caleb was able to rouse the people to action. In response to Joshua's speech, the people of the promise threatened to kill Joshua and Caleb.

As an executive coach and congregational consultant, I have repeatedly seen the impact of the pessimistic majority report. Denominational officials complete the demographic analysis, marketing experts apply their models, real estate buying patterns are weighed, the life-cycle theory applied, and the experts announce to the aging congregation that they will not survive.

Usually the explanation for a congregation's demise is that the surrounding community has become too *something*—too Roman Catholic, too Hispanic, too African-American, too elderly, too impoverished, too Pentecostal, too wealthy (it is as if "Nephilim" dwell in the land)—and the analysis predicts defeat.

The congregation is commended for their founding moments—their wonderful future is now behind them. I've attended the commemorative services where the history is recited, the former youth programs, the wonderful Christmas Eve services, the picnics, the Easter Sunrise Service, the bowling team, and the retreats all fondly remembered. Once upon a time, the congregation was building an identity, forming their bylaws, doing ministry, baptizing, marrying, comforting, educating, and burying; but now it is time, they are told, to hang it up.

Now, the congregation is doing little more than wandering through the wilderness. While there may be many rich and fulfilling opportunities for ministry, the majority report counsels against the risk, and the congregation whimpers into oblivion, choosing closure or hospice-like mission-funding (or worse yet, merger).

Most congregational leaders respond with the acquiescence of Moses and Aaron. They've been told it's not going to happen, so they slump into despair, update their resumes, attend a retreat for burned out leaders, or switch careers to interim ministry or insurance sales. Occasionally checking the budget, some pastors suggest that the congregation sell the manse or rent out space, raising sufficient cash to keep the congregation viable until the minister's retirement.

What confounded the imagination of the pessimistic spies in Kadesh were the same misperceptions that diminish the integrity of congregations today.

First, the ten spies perceived only the power of the enemies. Because the outward culture is bigger and stronger, because the competing affiliations are entrenched and better funded, it is presumed that a humble congregation cannot survive.

But the calculus for integrity does not see the environment as the enemy. Oriented Leaders see only the purpose of the mission and the promise to the people.

Joshua and Caleb were not intimidated by the Nephilim because the giants were not larger than the Covenant.

Second, the spies' pessimism confused institutional viability with mission. While the language refers to the closure of a church, the reality refers only to the shuttering of a building. The way in which congregations describe themselves, sets them up for this kind of thinking.

Too often the story of a congregation is told as a series of construction and remodeling projects, or the resumes of long-tenured pastors. Glory is remembered as a packed house or a dynamic preacher, but little is said about bodies and souls fed, wisdom's growth, or lives transformed. If the leadership considers only the physical characteristics of the institution and the personality of the preacher, then a pessimistic majority will kill imagination, and the spiritual possibility for the people is lost.

Hearing the integrity of Joshua and Caleb requires a whole new ear. It means to shift the people's attention from context to character, from intimidation to identity.

Joshua and Caleb did something only the greatest leaders accomplish, soemthing seldom appreciated in the moment by the majority. Joshua and Caleb chose to live their purpose.

Having left the Egyptian empire, the ten spies confused identity with infrastructure. They believed the power of Egypt was its imposing architecture, iron chariots, and civil administration. They followed Moses, driven by the promise of a national identity, but in the desert Peran they had built no pyramids, trained no war-horses, and developed no infrastructure. Without the trappings of accomplishment, the walled cities and neatly rowed farms of the Canaanites seemed to mock their rag-tag reality. Like a struggling congregation still using hymnals and cassette tapes in a Trinitron and pod-cast age, they counted themselves out.

But Joshua and Caleb saw something the people did not. These minority spies recognized that the children of Israel were in the wilderness for a single purpose—to move *through* the wilderness and arrive in the Promised Land. To pause, even for a moment, was to neglect more than opportunity. To pause was to concede the very identity of the people.

Moses had crushed the calf-god only weeks before, but its power still remained. The people of the Covenant, the inheritors of the Promised Land, the descendents of Abraham, Isaac, and Jacob, made a choice in Raphidim. They chose to be nomads rather than citizens. They abandoned their mission, because it seemed safer to live a wandering life without purpose than to risk a fight for meaning.

The failure to move forward to the Promised Land was to allow the calf-god of wandering to win. Bowing to the analysis which predicted failure idolized their enemies and sanctified their passivity.

Throughout the exodus, Joshua never deviated from this single purpose. He had come to move with the people *into* the Promised Land. Joshua gave no indication of doubt, confusion, or exhaustion. But there in the desert of Peran, when the people chose to abandon their identity, Joshua recognized both the inadequacy of their conviction and the weakness of Moses and Aaron's resolve.

Perhaps because the people didn't complain as much under Joshua's leadership as they did under Moses, we have no record of Joshua complaining to God about the kvetching of the people. On the other hand, perhaps the people didn't complain under Joshua's leadership *because* of Joshua's leadership. After the disaster at Raphidim, we have no recorded words of Joshua until the death of Moses. For the next 38 years, Joshua remained the silent third in command.

Even if they were to be crushed in the process of invasion (something neither Joshua nor Caleb could even imagine), they would rather die pursuing purpose than exist in dissolute safety. The tragedy of Kadesh in the desert of Peran was not a simple loss of nerve; it was the near annihilation of identity.

Caleb and Joshua predicted victory; but they saw their continued offensive not as the *better* choice. It was their *only* choice!

This is no new insight; congregations have turned before to the integrity of Joshua and Caleb, as expressed in the old gospel hymn: "Caleb Saw the Lord."[10]

1. Others saw the giants, Caleb saw the Lord;
They were sore disheartened, He believed God's word;
And that word he fully, fearlessly, obeyed—
Was it not sufficient that the Lord hath said?

Chorus
I will never leave thee;
Go in this thy might;
One shall chase a thousand,
Two put ten to flight.

2. O to follow fully like this one of old;
O to be like Caleb, doing what is told;
Then the Lord's rich blessing will be ours today,
He will prosper ever those who Him obey. *Chorus*

3. If we are half-hearted, we'll not taste God's best;
Those who follow wholly will be wholly blest,
Blest in soul and spirit, body, mind, and heart,
Rich in heav'nly treasure, which He will impart. *Chorus*

4. O to have one Master, only One to please;
O to have one purpose, not our will or ease;
Pressing ever onward to the goal before,
Serving gladly, wholly, Him whom we adore. *Chorus*

Amen.

---

[10]   "Caleb Saw the Lord" was a hymn my father used to sing. I have been unable to find any references for the author or composer.

PART II
JOSHUA'S LAST LECTURE

INTRODUCTION

After a long time had passed and the LORD had given
Israel rest from all their enemies around them, Joshua,
by then old and well advanced in years, summoned all
Israel—their elders, leaders, judges and officials—and
said to them: "I am old and well advanced in years. You
yourselves have seen everything the LORD your God
has done to all these nations for your sake; it was the
LORD your God who fought for you." [Joshua 23:1-3]

In a world seeking quick solutions to complex problems, listening to
elders is a waste of time. After all, when our elders were young they made the
choices that created today's problems. A culture that worships novelty abhors
experience!

The 23rd and 24th chapters of Joshua offer nothing but worn observations
from an ancient warrior. In the first three verses we are reminded of Joshua's
age no less than four times. (With wonderful redundancy, we are told Joshua
is not only old, he is also "well advanced in years", a phrase Joshua himself
repeats.)

In our culture referring to someone as "old" is an insult, but in Joshua's
context, advanced age gave credibility of the highest order. At issue was not the
chronological accumulation of years; anyone can pile up birthdays by not dying.
Joshua's advanced age was a compliment. Because he had seen the rhythms of
choice and consequence, Joshua could proclaim with confidence what his eyes
had witnessed and his heart had learned.

Only Joshua and Caleb could recall the Exodus from adult memory. Their
survival gave reliable witness to a people seeking orientation. The lessons of
the past were not single moments; the people did not affirm their identity once

and for all. The lessons of history were an ever-flowing sequence of decisions and outcomes, multiple moments when the Covenant would be affirmed or rejected. Joshua was a living witness to this cycle.

In the last two chapters of his book, Joshua declares his accumulated wisdom based upon the historic events of his life. These chapters are not stammering attempts to secure a legacy of personal accomplishment; they are simple observations of what Joshua learned from years of leadership through change, discipline, and integrity.

Listening carefully to Joshua's instruction is not the activity of sitting at the feet of an aged man, but listening instead to the living flow of history. Joshua had little interest in self-promotion; his only desire was to declare to the people how things worked. In the end, the message was not about *him*, it was about *them*.

This was the conclusion of the great warrior's time. Far behind were the days when Joshua was the finest spy in the intelligence branch of the Israeli army. Gone were the days when he and Caleb could scale walls with rope and grappling hook. Years had passed since Joshua could kill a man with his bare hands or inspire warriors to fight 'round the clock. Once, the bravest men wept at the privilege to serve, sweat, and possibly die under the honorable command of Joshua. Now, he was old and would never again hold his great javelin over the battlefield, shouting the war cry that would rouse entire armies into heroism beyond themselves.

Joshua had only one more speech to give, and he was going to make that speech again and again until the light would go from his eyes, hoping to pass a torch that would kindle an ongoing fire in the people's hearts. Joshua had one more speech, and he was going to deliver that speech until every man, woman, boy, and girl could speak it, feel it, and own it.

Joshua told the story because it was possible that some still did not "get it". It was possible that some still didn't have all the details. And Joshua knew someday the people would be asked their identity and if they did not know these stories, they would not survive.

In a single ten minute speech Joshua makes eight precise moves, each of which conveys a leadership principle to the landed children of Israel. And while his congregation's context is far removed from ours, his comprehension of the human condition echoes fresh hope for our future.

The following eight chapters are explorations of Joshua's eight leadership principles. At the end of each I have included ten discussion questions, believing Joshua's last lecture will convey hope for today's Joshua leaders.

CHAPTER 1

Assemble the Meeting

> Then Joshua assembled all the tribes of Israel at Shechem. He summoned the elders, leaders, judges and officials of Israel, and they presented themselves before God. (Joshua 24:1)

Meeting assembly is an acquired discipline well worth acquiring. No matter how great the speech, how informative the ensuing discussion, nothing undermines the resolve of decision making like the naysayers who failed to show up for the meeting.

Effective meetings begin with an inclusive invitation

From the beginning, inclusivity was important to Joshua. After the death of Moses, Joshua understood that only a tribal federation could conquer the Promised Land. This strategy required unity. As the book opens, the Reubenites, Gadites, and the half tribe of Manasseh were already home. Joshua's leadership convinces the militia of these two and a half tribes to fight on behalf of their brothers. As noted in Part I, the core of Joshua's first speech as commander (Joshua 1:12-15) was a call to inclusion. Joshua announced "No one is home until everyone is home."

Years later, the meeting at Shechem required representatives from every tribe, including Ephraim and the half-tribe of Menasha. Shechem was a long way from their home east of the Jordan, but the people knew Joshua was serious about his invitation; all were expected to attend.

Full assembly prevents destructive secrets and second-guessing. The whole body needs to be present when the life of the corporate assembly is at stake.

Effective meetings emphasize the importance of location

In this particular location, the children of Israel come full circle to the original promise given to Abraham in Genesis 12.

> So Abram left, as the LORD had told him; and Lot went with him. Abram was seventy-five years old when he set out from Haran. He took his wife Sarai, his nephew Lot, all the possessions they had accumulated and the people they had acquired in Haran, and they set out for the land of Canaan, and they arrived there.
>
> Abram traveled through the land as far as the site of the great tree of Moreh at Shechem. At that time the Canaanites were in the land. The LORD appeared to Abram and said, "To your offspring I will give this land." So he built an altar there to the LORD, who had appeared to him. (Genesis 12:4-6)

Imagine the significance! Every citizen having heard the story of the Covenant delivered to Abraham hundreds of years before, standing on the very soil where the promise was made. Those who gathered at Shechem were the living, physical fulfillment of the promise made to Abraham centuries before on that very spot! Assembly at Shechem was not one of convenience; it was of deep historic significance.

Many congregations gather surrounded by evidences of kept promises. Stained-glass windows, memorial plaques, cornerstones, dedication plates glued to the insides of pew Bibles and hymnals, all stand as silent sentries to the evidence of God's timeless Covenant.

Some pastors resist the roll call of the dead, feeling that they are constrained by the past every time they encounter another inscription dedicating some object to the memory of a long-forgotten parishioner. Quite the opposite is the case. These are not gatherings at the tombs of memory, but reminders of the continuity of promise. Gifts were made to honor some dimension of God's faithfulness expressed in the life of those so named.

Joshua's agenda was punctuated by the unmistakable memory of Abraham; the gathering was evidence that the original Covenant was very much alive. Shechem inspired connection, continuity, and accountability. Joshua had business to conduct with the descendents of Abraham, business that required their binding to what happened centuries before at that very place.

The evidence of fulfilled promises is a powerful tool, galvanizing identity for decision makers.

Effective meetings have clear agendum

Prior to the meeting in Joshua 24, Joshua had circulated his agenda to the people through the elders, leaders, judges, and officials recorded in chapter 23.

> After a long time had passed and the LORD had given Israel rest from all their enemies around them, Joshua, by then old and well advanced in years, summoned all Israel—their elders, leaders, judges and officials—and said to them: "I am old and well advanced in years." (Joshua 23:1-2)

What follows in Joshua 23 is the warrior's farewell address to his officers. It was a rousing recollection of vision, victory, and vigilance, but it was not a business meeting. It was a carefully crafted retirement address. The speech to his colleagues in chapter 23 became the agenda for Joshua's closing address and business meeting with the full membership in chapter 24.

Effective meetings respect member's input and time

I once served on the board of a not-for-profit organization where the president could barely gather a quorum for the annual business meeting. One year, following poor attendance at the board meeting, he announced to a gathering of the full membership that the eight board members who had bothered to come to the annual meeting voted to dissolve the organization and sell the property to the Mormons. While he was joking, the message was clear; if you can't gather the necessary representatives, effective action becomes difficult.

Poor attendance will be exploited by those wishing to undercut leadership's authority. Regardless of the polity, those who conduct business without the full participation of ratifying bodies do so to their own peril, risking not only their own authority but also the credibility of any future process.

Poor attendance seldom just "happens", it is trained. Absenteeism often reflects the attitude of leaders who fail to take participation seriously. The president who announced the sale of the organization to the Mormons, conducted meetings where descent was seldom permitted. Discussion was cut-off. Speakers for the opposition were ridiculed. Occasionally members with legitimate concerns were not even recognized by the chair.

Few wish to spend their time as stewards of the "rubber-stamp". Failure to conduct business in a fair and open manner usually results in chronic absenteeism. "Why bother, it won't make any difference," is frequently the cry of those absent. The best medicine for poor attendance is to hold meetings where full participation truly matters.

Recruitment, retention, and attendance of the best leaders, begins with an atmosphere of respect, not only for the participants' wisdom, but also their time. If there is little business to be conducted, the meetings should be brief. If there is a great deal of business, the conversation should be focused.

My own father, who needed to get up for work every morning around 4:30 AM, was frustrated when he served on his congregation's board where meetings would go well past midnight. On more than one occasion, he lamented, "The only person in that room who can sleep-in the next morning is the pastor, and he's the reason the meetings go so long!"

Effective meetings segregate social time

Meetings occasionally lose focus because those who gather find it as their only time to fellowship. Casual conversation becomes a part of the meeting because the members seldom have an opportunity to catch up with one another. Providing ample opportunity for conversation, independent from the business, usually improves the flow and duration of meetings.

One congregation I served had elders from different parts of the city who seldom met beyond coffee fellowship on Sundays. As a result, elder's meetings often took hours, not to conduct the business but to catch up on family news and life events. I finally addressed this problem by holding business meetings every other month alternating with bi-monthly fellowship meetings. While we conducted business half as frequently, these meetings became twice as efficient, seldom lasting longer than one hour.

Our fellowship meetings usually included a meal, party, or outing with spouses or guests. On one occasion we even went to dinner and the theater. During these gatherings, no business was conducted unless it was an absolute emergency. In five years no such emergency arose. We did, however, hold informal conversations about community needs, mission, vision, tone, and effectiveness.

The results were amazing. Prior to the alternating schedule, the elders met twelve times each year for a total of 36-40 hours. After the alternating schedule was implemented, the elders continued to meet twelve times each year, but the total number of hours met was less than 25, including our dinners and events. What's more, the group's productivity accelerated, individual members debated issues more freely, and nominations for new leaders became easier as the congregation heard how much the elders enjoyed their tenure.

Leaders who seek to break bad attendance habits must be willing to take their meetings seriously, even when other participants do not. A friend of mine who was made director of her division was frustrated by employees who were consistently late for weekly staff meetings. Her solution was to begin each meeting on time, regardless of who was present. At the beginning of the meeting, she reviewed project assignments and holiday schedules. When employees were held accountable for tasks for which they had not prepared, or came to work when the office was closed because they missed hearing the schedule, they quickly shifted their behavior. They soon started arriving for the beginning of staff meetings.

Training for effective meetings is worth the effort

By the time Joshua sent the summons to Shechem, the people had been well trained. They knew Joshua's meetings were important. Since the days of the Jericho parade-drills, the children of Israel knew their attendance was not optional, their time would be respected and their full attention was expected.

Whatever the polity, effective meetings require attendance. Building the priority of participation takes time, but it is time well spent, bolstering both the unity and commitment of the congregation.

The next principle in Joshua's last lecture is closely linked to his wisdom regarding location, it is a review of history.

Discussion Questions:

1) Who meets to conduct the business of your congregation?
2) How are they notified?
3) Where and when do they meet, and why?
4) Is there an agenda prepared?
5) Is the agenda followed?
6) Does the meeting time and place affirm authority or undermine it?
7) Where was your congregation founded?
8) What were the expectations of those who founded your congregation?
9) Are there memorials around your facilities? Who were these people?
10) How will future generations remember your leadership?

CHAPTER 2

Know Your History

Joshua said to all the people, "This is what the LORD, the God of Israel, says: 'Long ago your forefathers, including Terah the father of Abraham and Nahor, lived beyond the River and worshiped other gods. But I took your father Abraham from the land beyond the River and led him throughout Canaan and gave him many descendants. I gave him Isaac, and to Isaac I gave Jacob and Esau. I assigned the hill country of Seir to Esau, but Jacob and his sons went down to Egypt.

'Then I sent Moses and Aaron, and I afflicted the Egyptians by what I did there, and I brought you out. When I brought your fathers out of Egypt, you came to the sea, and the Egyptians pursued them with chariots and horsemen as far as the Red Sea. But they cried to the LORD for help, and he put darkness between you and the Egyptians; he brought the sea over them and covered them. You saw with your own eyes what I did to the Egyptians. Then you lived in the desert for a long time.

I brought you to the land of the Amorites who lived east of the Jordan. They fought against you, but I gave them into your hands. I destroyed them from before you, and you took possession of their land. When

Balak son of Zippor, the king of Moab, prepared to fight against Israel, he sent for Balaam son of Beor to put a curse on you. But I would not listen to Balaam, so he blessed you again and again, and I delivered you out of his hand.

'Then you crossed the Jordan and came to Jericho. The citizens of Jericho fought against you, as did also the Amorites, Perizzites, Canaanites, Hittites, Girgashites, Hivites and Jebusites, but I gave them into your hands. I sent the hornet ahead of you, which drove them out before you—also the two Amorite kings. You did not do it with your own sword and bow. So I gave you a land on which you did not toil and cities you did not build; and you live in them and eat from vineyards and olive groves that you did not plant." [Joshua 24:2-13]

W hen I was little, there was in our congregation an old friend of the family, Mr. Hyle, whom I thought was really cool. Well into his 80's, Mr. Hyle was funny, noted for his little comments about aging. I remember him telling me, "There are two things I don't like about getting old. First, I'm forgetful and I'm afraid I'm repeating myself, and second I keep repeating myself because I'm so forgetful."

History means redundantly repeating the story

Scripture tends to be redundant. Themes, stories, accounts are repeated again and again. Why all the reinforcement? Why four Gospels when one could have done the trick? Why so many accounts of the kings and how they were good or bad? Why so many prophets saying essentially the same thing over and over? And why is the account of the liberation from Egypt repeated *ad nauseum*.

As a pastoral counselor, I've discovered there are two primary reasons that family stories get repeated. First, there are multiple story tellers and each and every one wants to convey his or her version of events. One version of a story gets told, and another family member has to tell the same story to convey his or her perception and priorities. That seems to be what happened when we received four Gospels, each author providing a different slant on the telling.

The second reason people repeat themselves is because the listeners have not changed their behavior to confirm their understanding. When spouses argue and one or the other repeats the same story again and again, he or she is merely conveying that their partner still hasn't "got it". They repeatedly bring up old stories because their partner's behavior hasn't changed, even though the account is a cautionary tale, illustrating the depth of the problem. When a spouse complains to me that his or her partner keeps repeating the same story, I suggest that they won't move forward until they learn what the story is about.

This seems to be what is going on with the retelling of the Exodus. In Joshua 24 the ancient warrior stands before the people and tells the story—again. He speaks of the promise to Abraham, the call beyond the Euphrates. He talks about Isaac and Jacob and Joseph. He tells about the twelve brothers descending to Egypt, and the deliverance by Moses and Aaron. Joshua recalls the destruction of their enemies in the wilderness, and their arrival into the land with victory over Jericho. He reminds them how they were handed a homeland ready-made, with houses built by others, vineyards pre-planted, and farmland already tilled for planting.

These were familiar stories repeated until the people could lip-sync with the speaker. As Joshua drove home the point, these stories were not distant remembrances of a people long gone; these were *their* stories. They confirmed the continuity and identity of a people once lost to slavery, then found wandering, and now rooted in a Promised Land.

Joshua repeated himself in chapters 23 and 24, almost word for word, in the recollection of the Covenant, Exodus, and Conquest. He did so in the voice of an old man, prone to repetition. Joshua recounted the stories to them as if their very life as a people depended upon their hearing them again, because it did!

Joshua's telling of the story was selective. In forging the identity of the people, he did not choose to tell of the Golden Calf, the rejection of Caleb's spy report, the kvetching for water, or longing for slave food. Instead Joshua chose to tell the story of God's faithfulness to the people's best choices. And what we choose to speak about our history shapes our future.

History means repeating the important parts again

One extremely successful synagogue in Chicago had developed a reputation for being an unusually liberal community.

The Rabbi who presided over much of the congregation's growth had begun serving the community at a time of severe decline. Many members believed he would be the congregation's last Rabbi, providing competent care until closure or merger with another synagogue. This Rabbi, however, began to read the synagogue's history. In it he discovered the roots of a progressive forward-thinking congregation.

He began to highlight his synagogue's liberal identity in weekly sermons, monthly newsletters, and conversations with leadership. He held before them their identity as an "out-of-the-box" Jewish community. Whenever he spoke of the congregation, he did not describe their recent decline, but instead recounted their much longer tradition of liberalism and growth.

He never missed an opportunity to discuss the progressive elements of their history, often pointing out that they were the first synagogue in the United States to allow a woman to address a Sabbath service. He justified the tradition-breaking theology of his synagogue by using their own history, which included Jane Addams addressing the congregation regarding female reproductive rights shortly after the turn of the 20th century.

Soon, when most urban synagogues were in decline or closing, this community was receiving new members, including converts, at a record pace, growing from a few dozen to several thousand. They even constructed the first new synagogue facility in Chicago's city limits in over two decades, because their leader spoke the elements of their history which forged the strongest identity.

History means finding the verbs

Congregational histories are usually written for the sake of an anniversary, building dedication, or pastor's retirement. Occasionally they are trotted out for the new member's class or handed to the consultant interested in such esoterica. But in the drive toward the future, leaders often miss the power of history.

Usually the power is lost because the stories are told in a distancing way. An outline of building projects or the *vitae* of former pastors tells the congregation little about *their* identity. Reading the account of a groundbreaking ceremony for a building which is now in disrepair tends to highlight the shortages of the present. Hearing the success of pastors long dead can make a people wistful for the giftedness of former leaders. How leaders tell the story effects *what* the people learn.

Joshua did not memorialize the patriarchs. His speech was not about the nobility of Abraham, or the wisdom of Joseph. Joshua did not discuss the courage of Moses or the superior strength of the soldiers, now dead, who defeated the Amorites. No, Joshua's words were quotes from an active God, who was present in the past and equally present for the future. These were not stories of things that happened a long time ago, this was a single account with several illustrations of God's perpetual action.

At every turn, Joshua's history lesson made YHWH the actor. A simple summary of the verbs in the English translation illustrates the dynamic activity of this deity: took, led, gave, assigned, sent, afflicted (the Egyptians), brought, etc.

These powerful verbs of God's activity bound the Israelites to a past that could define their every present moment. Abraham, Isaac, Jacob, Moses, and

Aaron were dead, and if the people needed their kind of leadership in order to thrive, they were sunk. But because their possibilities were given by an ever-present God, then power for the future could not diminish.

Joshua understood how history is a present participant at every table. In the Maggid, the telling of the Exodus is recited as part of the Passover Haggadah. The first person, not the third person, pronoun is used in the mealtime liturgy to recount God's activity:

> **We** were slaves to Pharaoh in Egypt, and the Lord, our God, took **us** out from there with a strong hand and with an outstretched arm. If the Holy One, blessed be He, had not taken our fathers out of Egypt, then we, our children and our children's children would have remained enslaved to Pharaoh in Egypt. (Excerpted from *The Passover*, Kehot Publication Society, Brooklyn NY)

Effective congregational histories are owned by the present congregation. They are recited, spoken, and remembered as the identity of the people speaking. They are not academic codifications of the past; they are mnemonic tools for the present.

The power of the story is not found in what *was* accomplished, but in the example of what *can* happen—verbs of God's activity.

Joshua was, of course, setting the stage. He knew the identity of the people was at stake. Without a shared history, their capacity to unite and endure would disappear. They were twelve tribes divided by a river. Joshua was aware that the northern-most tribes of Dan, Asher, and Naphtali would be trading with the Phoenician empire. If they could not connect to the identity of Joseph's brothers, they would be absorbed by the prevailing culture.

Divided congregations tend to have divided histories, recounting ethnic, theological, or cultural fissures in their past. These fissures in memory lead to continued permission for dissension. Denominations founded as off-shoots from other denominations are prone to subdividing because their history warrants schism as a means to resolve conflict. Both unity and division are learned. Accounts of past resolution and reconciliation become the reason for continued engagement and accommodation; whereas accounts of past division justify present and future schism.

History, properly told, pulls the thread of identity through the tapestry of the past into the craft of present struggle and beyond to the design of the future. Joshua understood the power of history, not told to embellish what *was*, but to empower what *is*.

History is told for the sake of the future

I once had the pleasure of attending the transfer of property from an elderly white congregation to a growing black congregation on Chicago's south-side. For many the transfer was reason for concern, as it was the first African-American institution to take residence in a predominantly Caucasian area of the community. Some angry whites wrote nasty letters to the leadership of the selling congregation, claiming they were about to destroy their neighborhood, but the aging leadership held firm, knowing that two dozen members could no longer care for the property.

Members of the black congregation also had reservations. One older member told the pastor it would be difficult for him to attend church in a neighborhood where, as a child, he was forbidden to go. Even though the move was only a few blocks from their original location, it was, for many, worlds away.

The service of transfer was well attended and celebratory. A beautiful facility would house a new congregation, and the departing congregation would receive sufficient compensation for the sale. They would not disband; they could continue to worship in a rented facility.

Hymns were sung, sermons delivered; some wept, all smiled. But the most powerful moment in this service of dedication was when the pastor of the new occupants recounted the history of the departing people.

This had been the location of great things! Colonel George Clarke and Sarah Dunn, founders of Chicago's Pacific Garden Mission, had been members of the departing congregation. William Jennings Bryant once preached from that very pulpit. Pastors, professors, missionaries, and scholars had received their confirmation as children in the classrooms of that building. The bricks and mortar bore witness to the faithfulness of a powerful God who worked through the people within those walls.

The pastor's words ended with a pledge to continue the faithful stewardship of what had begun in that place over 120 years before. He promised their ministry would be a continuation of what had always happened at that address. God's work, through a people who called that building their congregation's home, would continue unabated.

History had power that day! Words of history, properly told, united two congregations from two sides of a community, representing two different denominations and cultures. But in that place there was to be only one history, the activity of *one* God.

How leadership chooses to tell the story of a people lays the foundation for their future.

Discussion Questions:

1) What need was being met by the founders of your congregation?
2) How did they choose to meet that need?
3) What obstacles has God overcome for your congregation?
4) Where did the "hornet go ahead of you?" (See: Joshua 24:12)
5) When have the people of your congregation rebelled?
6) What was the price of their rebellion?
7) When have they been most faithful?
8) What are the surrounding evidences of God's faithfulness to past members of your congregation? (e. g. property, building, furnishings, curriculum, endowment, a working kitchen, etc.)
9) Would your congregation's history read differently if God were the primary subject?
10) What past victories illustrate how God may be assisting you now?

CHAPTER 3

Articulate the Options

"Now fear the LORD and serve him with all faithfulness. Throw away the gods your forefathers worshiped beyond the River and in Egypt, and serve the LORD. But if serving the LORD seems undesirable to you, then choose for yourselves this day whom you will serve, whether the gods your forefathers served beyond the River, or the gods of the Amorites, in whose land you are living." [Joshua 24:14-15]

It takes confidence for leaders to allow the congregation to consider the alternatives which contradict the leaders' values. Oriented Leaders are not intimidated when followers weigh their options. Insecure leaders limit the group's ability to imagine their freedom *not* to follow. Meetings are poorly run, motions are quickly passed, and adjournment occurs without reflection. When challenged, insecure leaders present issues as if there were only two options; black or white, feast or famine, right or wrong, good or evil, their way or the highway. Over time the rank and file feels railroaded.

A choice isn't a choice unless you can choose

Joshua understood the importance of the decision the nation was about to make. They were about to choose their god(s) which would organize every dimension of their communal life. This decision was so important Joshua knew that the people needed the freedom to consider all of the alternatives.

Transparency regarding viable options requires confidence borne of low anxiety. A limited range of choices posted as polar-opposites only confirms the reality of anxious leaders.

When leaders present opposing viewpoints without anxiety, both leaders and congregations better trust the decision made. But when the options presented imply dire outcomes, the decision creates resentment as the group's decision is made under pressure to comply.

When it came to picking a deity, Joshua had a sense of proportion. He was able to articulate alternatives because, while he knew what was at stake for the people, he was not the least bit insecure about what was at stake for him.

Joshua knew his own orientation, so he was able to permit the luxury of multiple-choice. And because Joshua presented the options in an environment of inclusion, historical-context, and fairness, he was willing to allow the congregation the risky opportunity to make up their own minds!

In verses 2-13, Joshua concluded his review of YHWH's benefits. On the basis of this argument alone he could have reasonably enforced *his* religion on the people, but Joshua did not believe *deum rex est deum publicus* (the god of the king is the god of the people). The choice of a national deity was not a decision Joshua would make on their behalf. Instead he put before them reasonable options and the freedom to choose a god for themselves. Even though the ancient warrior had won the battles, Joshua knew it was possible to lose the people.

A choice isn't a choice if the alternatives are foolish

I have heard otherwise rational people make extreme statements in order to sway the group's decision. "We either adopt this program or the church will close!" or "Without a contemporary worship alternative many families in our community will never hear about Jesus!" or "If we don't fund the youth group ski trip we're saying it's okay for teenagers who would have accepted Christ to die and go to hell!"

I have also witnessed more than one meeting where the deck was "stacked". Leaders provided a limited range of options manipulating the outcome to their desire. One congregation, when preparing to change its name, offered for membership vote only two choices. The first, clearly the preference of the board, had a familiar "Christ's Church" kind of feel. The second option was a difficult, cumbersome name with a cultish ring, something like "The Holy Church of Only Those Who Trust in Jesus". (It is easy to guess which option won the vote.)

Likewise, I have seen decisions manipulated by calling for votes based on so little data that opposition was made to appear foolish. One congregation was asked to terminate a staff member's contract based on "concerns" which the pastor refused to actuate. When the members asked for additional information the chair sited issues of confidentiality. When the staff member requested further investigation into the unspoken allegations, he was ruled out of order for making a motion as a non-member. Those who attempted to speak on behalf of retaining the staff member were criticized for not having all the information. In the end the contract was not renewed, but the whole matter was challenged in civil court leaving the congregation to pay substantial compensation to the terminated employee.

A reasonable presentation of choice permits full exploration of the options. At Shechem Joshua suggested three viable alternatives for divine worship: the gods worshiped in Egypt, the patron gods of their new homeland, or YHWH whom the nation had known for a generation. The people understood the implications of each.

To adopt the Egyptian deities of their grandparents would tie them to their slave-dwelling heritage. These gods had sustained the Israelites through centuries of oppression. Continued allegiance would respectfully memorialize the suffering in the house of bondage. To keep the gods of their Egyptian slave-camps would connect the nation to their ancestors buried in Egyptian soil.

Adoption of the local Amorite deities was equally logical, after all these were the gods who had blessed the land with milk and honey. Acculturation to a new environment could reasonably mean adaptation to local custom. Perhaps the Israelite victory over the Amorites was proof the local gods liked the new residents and looked forward to Israeli devotees.

Joshua's fair and open presentation of the options required trust. Disentangling his personal preference from congregational choice permitted Joshua the ability to reasonably convey the options. But Joshua's trust was not a belief that God's Spirit would work effectively through the voice of the people. Joshua's choice to provide a fair representation of the alternatives was possible because he trusted himself when faced with the possibility of loss.

Stacking the deck or sequestering discussion is another sure sign of insecure leadership. Leaders who lack confidence in the validity of their own choice, or lack the courage to maintain their orientation if they do not get their way, create secrecy and manipulation.

Joshua remained confident *not* because he believed the *people* would do the "right thing", Joshua remained confident because he knew *he* would do the right thing regardless of what the people chose.

A choice isn't a choice unless you're willing to lose

When faced with losing the vote, leaders have only three healthy options. First, leaders can submit to the will of the people, thereby affirming their commitment to due process rather than preferred outcomes. Second, they can resign from leadership, recognizing their preferred direction is more important than their continued authority. Third, they can incite rebellion, insisting on both the superiority of their judgment and their right to lead.

There is a fourth unhealthy option too frequently exercised. Finding themselves on the losing side of an issue, leaders remain in authority offering public support of the people's choice, but quietly sabotaging the group's ability to implement their decisions. More often than not, stagnant congregations are led by individuals who have chosen this path. Over time such inconsistency withers the coherence and will of an organization.

We do not know what Joshua would have done had the people chosen gods other than YHWH. Given what we do know about the great warrior we can presume he would have either washed his hands of the people's apostasy, or raised an army to protect a faithful remnant of Covenant citizens. But passive compliance to preserve his general's pension was not an option.

A choice isn't a choice until the leaders are confident

Years before, at the beginning of the conquest, Joshua understood the orientation of his values. Some decisions required acquiescence to the integrity of the process. Joshua maintained the treaty with the Gibeonites even when it was secured under false pretense (Joshua 9 and 10). Joshua also remained quietly resigned to decisions made by Moses with which he disagreed (Numbers 11), and was willing to openly confront opposition when he knew decisive action was required (Joshua 7). We clearly know Joshua would rather resign his commission than keep his job and compromise his Covenant values.

Oriented Leaders must trust themselves and their commitments. At some point the congregation's decision may diverge so significantly from the leader's values that continued leadership is no longer a viable option. Openly and fairly presenting choices requires leaders to understand their limits prior to the vote.

Discussion Questions:

1) Who makes the decisions for your congregation?
2) Where is opposition permitted?
3) What happens to individuals or groups when they lose a vote?
4) Have there been decisions made in which no action has followed?
5) Have there been occasions when leaders have been "voted down"?
6) If so, how did the leaders respond to the group's decision?

7) How does your congregation determine the seriousness of a particular issue?
8) What decisions have you supported even when you lost the vote?
9) How have you shown support for decisions with which you disagree?
10) As a leader, what decisions could lead you to resign?

CHAPTER 4

Declare Your Own Position

"But as for me and my household, we will serve the LORD." [Joshua 24:15b]

L eaders burn-out when the energy they expend fails to move them closer to the goals they desire.

This fact is easily understood when purchasing a large-ticket item over time, like a car. The first few payments seem manageable because they are going towards a brand new vehicle. But after a year or two, the payments are more difficult to make because the car is older and paying off the loan seems far away as most of the payment goes towards interest and the principle seems to diminish by just pennies. But on the back-side of the loan, when most of the payment brings down the remaining principle, the payments seem easier even though throughout the life of the loan the payments are exactly the same. Moving closer to the goal of payoff, the bills just don't seem as high.

You won't know *what* to do till you know *who* you serve

It is in the relationship between effort and goal achievement where most leaders make their mistakes. They tend to assume that the problem is with the energy expended not the goal itself. Whether they work harder or smarter, if the effort is applied to a goal about which the leaders do not care, leaders will burn out.

Joshua knew the value of leadership was not found in how hard he worked to convince the people to follow. Leadership meant knowing where he was going to invest *his* energy before the people made their decision.

"But as for me and my household, we will serve the LORD," is the most significant sentence in the entire book of Joshua. Joshua's strength and bravery in command, his willingness to speak truth to power, his unbending approach to discipline, and his unwavering commitment to integrity, boil down to a single fact. Joshua knew *whom he was going to serve.* True leadership begins with the capacity to understand one's own following. Undistracted by the choice of the crowd, Joshua made his decision to serve the Lord regardless of popular whim or response.

Don't poll the audience, know your answer

Surveys are a clear sign that the leadership of a congregation has become unclear on their personal goals. "Let's ask the congregation what they want, so we know what to do!" While this thought seems so inclusive, it communicates to the membership two things about their leadership.

First, surveys tend to demonstrate that the leaders are out of touch. Unclear about the attitudes and expectations of the people they serve, leaders turn to questionnaires in order to cater to the group's agenda. Second, surveys abdicate the leaders' responsibility to set a course. Having no clue regarding where to go next, survey results become a convenient way to hide from decisive orientation. If the next program fails, leadership can blame the rank and file for choosing the direction, rather than taking responsibility for setting the course.

The other problem with surveys is how people lie. When asked, most congregations will overwhelmingly respond that they want to learn more about theology and the Bible. When the classes are scheduled, however, attendance seldom reflects the statistical enthusiasm.

Truly Oriented Leadership begins with truly Oriented Leaders.

The story is told of St. Francis of Assisi who was hoeing his garden one afternoon. He was asked by a novitiate, "What would you do if you were suddenly to learn that you were to die at sunset today?" He replied, "I would finish hoeing my garden."

Believing the task at hand fits into an unwavering purpose orients leadership well beyond any focus-group data.

A simple question measures the true orientation of leaders. If nobody was following, would you still be walking the same path? *Leading requires followers, orientation does not.*

Joshua was perfectly willing *not* to lead. In fact it was more important to maintain his orientation to God's service than to convince the people where to go. This is why Joshua announces *his* decision *before* the people weigh-in with their decision. Joshua wanted to be completely clear about what he was going to do next rather than change his course to stay with the people.

While counseling burned-out pastors, I have discovered the single common denominator underlying their exhaustion was their decision to follow the congregation's will in order to stay in charge rather than follow their own calling. This does not mean they necessarily compromised their morals or ethics; sometimes the choices of the group are appropriate for the congregation. What happens when the pastor burns out is a miss-fit between the direction of the congregation and the God-given capacities of the leader. Leaders with sustained energy for the long haul know who they are going to be with or without the congregation's vote.

Knowing your answer avoids the traps of technique

Oriented Leaders maintain a vision beyond the disposition of the group. Throughout the Book of Joshua his orientation towards an eternal value keeps both Joshua and the people from becoming trapped by "technique". Joshua never becomes a compliant tool of the people's expectations, nor are they compelled to be puppets of Joshua's agenda.

Compliant or compelling techniques are similar in that goals for the group or the leader become derivative; they arise solely from the leader, complying with the group's ideas or compelling the group to execute the leader's agenda. As a result, independent free-willed participation becomes impossible and everyone becomes either the manipulator or the manipulated.

A compliant technique (Fig. 1) requires the group to determine the goals; the leader only waits to facilitate whatever the group decides. Some seminaries even teach a compliant technique for ministry, suggesting pastors are to encourage visions and goals within the congregation and then provide their guidance and encouragement facilitating the people to accomplish whatever their goals may be.

The compliant leader forces the group to identify their goals through whatever means. Then, affirming their allegiance to the group, the leader moves them toward their goals without any real commitment to the direction. The leader remains "goal neutral", always ready to serve the will of the community.

Figure 1: The dysfunctional triangle of Compliant Technique

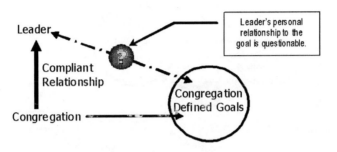

The compliant technique triangles the leader between the group and their goals

This was the leadership employed by Aaron at the base of Mt. Sinai. When the people came to him and requested a calf-god he was all too willing to bow to their wishes (Exodus 32:1-4). As a compliant leader, Aaron obliged.

A compelling technique (Fig. 2) is rooted in the manipulative relationship between the leader and the group. In this method leaders are expected to set the agenda, and then use their relationship with the group to compel movement. The goal requires resources, money, workers, mailing lists, etc., from the followers, but the group is not necessarily committed to the goal; their allegiance is to the leader.

This tends to be the style employed by the stereotypical televangelist. Followers send contributions to whatever project is being touted by the preacher, not because they believe in the project, but because they find the evangelist personally compelling. The goal could be a hospital, a school, keeping kids off drugs, or building a Christian amusement park; to the donors it makes no difference, just so long as they feel good about their relationship to the leader.

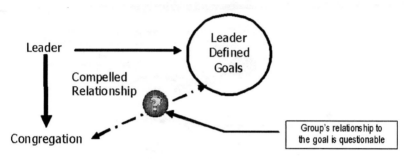

Figure 2: The dysfunctional triangle of
Compelling Technique

*The compelled technique triangles the group
between the leader and the leader's goals*

This was the leadership style employed by Moses when he came down from Mt. Sinai and found the people worshiping the calf-god. Moses defined the goals and aggressively compelled the people into submission. While Moses did end their apostasy, they did not turn away from the idol because they had changed; they turned out of sheer terror of the Levites' swords (Exodus 32:25-28).

Knowing your answer means you'll know what to ask

Joshua's Oriented Leadership (Fig. 3) permitted an unencumbered call for people to respond to the *goal*, not to him. Because Joshua knew the orientation of his life he could pursue his calling without needing to manipulate or facilitate the congregation.

Figure 3: Oriented Leadership differentiates between Self, Goals, & Group

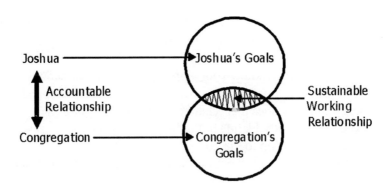

Before leaders can manage a congregation, they must first manage themselves. The discipline and integrity necessary for leadership begins with a personal commitment to know one's own orientation. The capacity to remain non-anxious in the face of the congregation's free will requires an unyielding confidence in one's own will.

Confident leaders are often accused of being uncaring, aloof, and callous to the needs of the group. Such accusations usually arise when the leaders refuse to allow the group's anxiety to shift their position from accountable to accommodating. Such complaints should not deter leaders from pursuing goals they know to be right. In the end, what may appear to be detachment is, in reality, clarity. Such clarity prevents manipulation and allows leaders to adopt Joshua's next leadership principle, rejecting false enthusiasm.

Discussion Questions:

1) In your congregation, when have there been tensions between the membership's and the leadership's goals?
2) How are these differences addressed?
3) What does your congregation expect from its leaders; compliance, compelling technique, or a clear articulation of the options and their leader's position?
4) Do you know where your leaders stand before a decision is made?
5) As a leader, how do you reenergize your personal priorities and focus?
6) As a leader do you know your abilities, goals, and direction?
7) If you are currently feeling burned-out, where are you spending your energy and how does that relate to your personal goals?
8) If you are currently feeling burned-out, what needs to shift, your goals or your relationship to the group?
9) Are there times when the group's decision means you should reorient your goals?
10) What would you do differently if the group would support you?

CHAPTER 5

Reject False Enthusiasm

Then the people answered, "Far be it from us to forsake the LORD to serve other gods! It was the LORD our God himself who brought us and our fathers up out of Egypt, from that land of slavery, and performed those great signs before our eyes. He protected us on our entire journey and among all the nations through which we traveled. And the LORD drove out before us all the nations, including the Amorites, who lived in the land. We too will serve the LORD, because he is our God."

Joshua said to the people, "You are not able to serve the LORD. He is a holy God; he is a jealous God. He will not forgive your rebellion and your sins." [Joshua 24:16-19]

I magine bringing the congregation to the culmination of a great decision. Imagine speaking so eloquently that the opposition stands teary-eyed, gape-mouthed, and in complete agreement with *you*. Imagine moving for the vote in a duly-called, well-executed meeting. Imagine the unanimous vote, the whole assembly applauding the wisdom of your proposal, cheering the passing of *your* resolution! Then imagine demanding a recount.

Know the difference between agreement and support

The power of persuasion can be dangerous. Leaders who bring success receive the adulation of the people; but there is a difference between appreciation and participation. Real commitment is not proved by a single vote or created by an enthusiastic rally; true commitment is confirmed by the people's actions *following* the meeting.

At Shechem the people voted before they discussed the motion. Joshua wanted to fully disclose the consequences of their decision before he could trust the vote. Oriented Leaders eye enthusiasm with suspicion. That is why Robert's Rules for Order places disclosure and discussion prior to the vote. Getting a motion passed is easy, getting the people moving is hard.

During a leadership retreat my congregation's elders and deacons pledged full support for expanded youth ministry. We had purchased a curriculum which would require extensive changes in our congregation's focus and a deep commitment from our leaders. A few staff and congregation members had attended training seminars for the implementation of this dynamic program. I was excited.

Our new focus on youth ministry required adjustments to every dimension of congregational life. Worship, fellowship, calendar, building use, and volunteer coordination changed to accommodate a new orientation to the young people from our community. Our Thursday night youth program grew from a half dozen disinterested teenagers to over forty high school students sharing music, games, dinner, and Bible study. The staff and a small handful of members were fully committed; but of those involved in the program, only one was from the twenty leaders who had voted for our new direction.

I continued to push for greater involvement from our leadership core. Every elder's meeting they would affirm their belief in our new direction, but every youth-night they failed to appear. I had confused formal enthusiasm *for* youth programming with active commitment *to* youth programming.

In an attempt to discern the congregation's support for our new direction, a core of those deeply involved with the youth developed a series of forums to re-present the program to leaders and members. As pastor I chose not to participate in these discussions. I had become suspicious that my own enthusiasm overshadowed honest opposition. My suspicions were correct. Over ninety percent of the active members attended at least one youth ministry forum. The attendees responded with a resounding "NO" to the changes this expanded programming required.

Dispassionately I presented the results to the congregational leadership. In a near unanimous vote, they decided to reverse their course and return to a quiet domesticated youth group. While the larger community had responded well to the new program, our leadership was not prepared to sustain significant change. In less than two months youth attendance dropped to less than twelve.

Rather than being frustrated by their withdrawal, I was grateful for their honesty.

What had developed during our brief foray into active youth ministry was a dissonance between the leadership's words and actions. I found this dissonance exhausting because I continued to treat the leaders as if they were "on-board" when clearly they were not. They in turn, affirmed our new direction verbally but without the kind of passion necessary to integrate new young people into the life of the congregation.

The losers in this deception were the youth themselves who were told how important they were to the congregation when, in reality, they were valued by only a few. To counter this dissonance I had found myself making excuses for the leaders—they were busy, they meant well, they were working in other areas so I could focus on the youth program—none of this was true.

After the leadership re-voted I no longer needed to explain their absence. We all became honest about the congregation's priorities. Honesty does not always bring what is hoped, but it always brings freedom from pretense.

It was then that I learned the difference between leaders who sponsor ideas and leaders who perform ministry.

At Shechem Joshua demanded honesty. At this point in his career, Joshua knew the power of his personality could carry a majority vote regardless of what he proposed. He had, after all, delivered them into the Promised Land, and their great gratitude afforded great latitude. But once again this issue was not about Joshua, it was about the people. *They* were going to have to live with the consequences of their decision. A euphoric affirmation of ideas would not be sufficient to sustain their choice into the future.

Know the difference between vanity and vitality

Like all great leaders, Joshua had little interest in the people's vote; he was concerned about their vitality. Verbal assent to YWHW's direction, without a corresponding transformation of behavior, would have destroyed the integrity of the nation, in direct violation of the third commandment:

> Thou shalt not take the name of the LORD thy God in vain; for the LORD will not hold him guiltless that taketh his name in vain. (Exodus 20:7 KJV)

The use of God's name to make the people "look" good was the height of vanity. Oriented Leaders reject as vain the verbal allegiance to The Divine unless there is wholehearted commitment in action to support the words.

In addition to being their first leader in the Promised Land, at Shechem Joshua became their first prophet. He stood at the beginning of a long line of inspired voices who denounced passive lip-service to faithfulness.

Leaders must be willing to re-visit decisions which are not backed-up by action. Oriented Leaders understand congregational vitality is a measure of trajectory—both direction and movement.

Joshua rejected the first response of the people because he knew they had acted impulsively. They had not carefully weighted the consequence of their decision.

Discussion Questions:

1) Looking at your congregation's mission statement, what are the stated priorities?
2) How are your stated priorities reflected in your congregational calendar?
3) How are they expressed in the order of worship?
4) When your leadership takes a vote, how does the discussion take place?
5) Does the discussion include a full disclosure of the consequences of both action and inaction?
6) Are some individual's motions more likely to pass than others simply because of who has presented the idea?
7) Has your congregation ever taken on a project or program which "failed"?
8) Why or why not?
9) When proposals do not meet the expectation of the congregation, how are the issues re-visited?
10) Are there places where you may be using God's name for vain purpose?

CHAPTER 6

Articulate the Consequences

"If you forsake the LORD and serve foreign gods, he will turn and bring disaster on you and make an end of you, after he has been good to you."

But the people said to Joshua, "No! We will serve the LORD."

Then Joshua said, "You are witnesses against yourselves that you have chosen to serve the LORD."

"Yes, we are witnesses," they replied.

"Now then," said Joshua, "throw away the foreign gods that are among you and yield your hearts to the LORD, the God of Israel." [Joshua 24:20-23]

A friend of mine works in an office in downtown Chicago. Her office currently looks out over a construction project, a brand new luxury hotel. When construction began she was frustrated, it blocked her view of the Chicago skyline. A few weeks later, however, she learned that the project underway was an award winning piece of architecture. Artist's renderings of the final structure shifted her opinion slightly, and she admitted to looking forward to seeing the final product.

Five months into construction the developer ran out of credit. The financing for this particular project was sufficient, but the failure of another property created a cascading disaster for the developer. Now my friend has not only lost her view of the skyline, she looks into the concrete and steel shell of a sixteen-story un-kept promise.

Calculate the cost before making the commitment

"What will happen if we sign-on? What will be required of us? What will be the evidence of our success?"

Oriented Leaders provide every opportunity for an honest buy-in by clearly answering these questions. As Jesus said, "before you build a tower or before you go to war, count the cost." (Luke 14:28-33) Carefully "counting the cost" was Christ's metaphor for fully informed personal commitment. Careful cost accounting is an organization's evidence of a fully informed future.

Joshua's words were a brief declaration of accounting. To buy-in with the YHWH-God was a total investment. If the nation was going to hedge against loss by diversifying their religious portfolio, they would come to ruin. Joshua understood the folly of leveraged commitment. Duplicitous accounting brings congregations down.

Cost accounting for ministry simply connects the balance sheet to balanced hearts. As the Proverbs state,

Honest scales and balances are from the LORD; all the weights in the bag are of his making. (Proverbs 16:11) and

Differing weights and differing measures—the LORD detests them both. (Proverbs 20:10)

At Shechem, Joshua was not merely telling the people to bring their regular offerings to the tabernacle in order to keep the tent-flaps open. Joshua's accounting regarded the full commitment of the people in how they would use power, property, and produce to maintain the faithfulness of the whole congregation. Oriented Leadership challenges the people to connect their vision to their values, their treasury to the treasured.

Joshua properly understood that the difficulty was not in establishing a commitment to YHWH; the difficulty was in insisting upon a total rejection of the alternatives. Oriented Leaders hold before the congregation their free option to follow, but they also must inform the congregation of the cost necessary to make the journey, and the greatest cost lies in what must be neglected in order to wholeheartedly continue. *Every "yes" to a new direction, requires a "NO" to every other direction.*

Removing duplicity is not easy. Occasionally a group will suggest a simple path to rid an organization of self-contradiction. Divesting a congregation's portfolio of corporations which do business in totalitarian countries, or replacing light bulbs with green efficient compact-fluorescents may seem like coherent choices, but such projects are only the beginning if a congregation takes seriously their commitment to "counting the cost".

Accounting for commitment begins with the ability to interpret a congregation's current location. I am amazed by the number of pastors who have no idea how to read a balance-sheet. Familiarity with simple principles of accounting should be basic instruction for individuals managing any not-for-profit corporation; pastors should be no exception. I have had conversations with too many church treasurers frustrated by their pastor's inability to produce original receipts for reimbursement. Accountability begins with the details; and the simplest, most measurable details begin with accurate financial records.

A clear understanding of membership-rolls, attendance, participation, and other congregational data is crucial when reviewing the condition of a congregation. These are the most measurable elements in interpreting a congregation's position, but these numbers must be understood as windows into deeper reflections of the membership's character. Accurately interpreting these elements requires great courage on the part of leaders who wish to convey the consequences.

Divest from all distractions

At one stewardship committee meeting I suggested a lack of giving was not the problem, it was the number of new cars in our parking lot and the amount of consumer debt in the credit card statements of our members. The anger I encountered after my off-handed comment indicated I had hit a nerve. "How dare I challenge the member's priorities? I had no right to call into question their financial choices!"

Likewise a group of parents came to me with their frustration that I wouldn't teach confirmation class at another time because it conflicted with hockey practice. I responded that life was about choices and they needed to consider if they were sending the right message to their children every time they drove them to hockey rather than confirmation. They were absolutely dumbfounded when I called the hockey coach and asked if he could move the practice time because it interfered with confirmation class. Again, I was told I had no right to interfere with the importance of sports, even though the hockey coach graciously moved the time of practice.

To presume spiritual matters are far too private to be encumbered by practical evidence separates real-world application from spiritual ideals. Joshua fully anticipated his challenge would result in the people physically removing foreign idols from their houses; the commitment of their hearts would be proven by the evidence in their dumpsters!

For Joshua, idols not removed from the people's homes would not be tolerated as an absent minded oversight; they would be interpreted as willful apostasy. It's leadership's responsibility to evaluate the quality of the people's following, not the congregation's.

Capitalize only your calling

Measuring the quality of a congregation's commitment begins with an inspection of their individual choices, but it also extends to their corporate priorities.

I had the pleasure of visiting one congregation that had sold its building and moved into a rented gymnasium. The decision was made when the trustees noted they were spending more money on building upkeep than on mission to the community. They were not dwindling in attendance, in fact they were growing, but they recognized that the priority of the congregation to minister to their neighborhood was limited by the constant expense of upkeep. With the proceeds from the sale of the building they were able to endow their rental expenses and use 100% of the weekly offerings for direct ministry. Using this money they purchased a small functional building that housed office space, a tutoring program, a community food pantry, and a youth center that welcomed kids off the streets. The pastor told me how little he missed having to wait for repairmen or inspecting the sanctuary to be sure it was clean. Having said "no" to a building, they were able to say "yes" to so much more.

In the process of moving from ownership to rental, the congregation lost several families. The pastor comfortably indicated they had transferred their membership to other congregations. He continued to visit each family until they assured him they were attending elsewhere. But for every family that had left, their new mission brought in four new families committed to the congregation's new direction.

Challenging congregations to consider the expression of their priorities will not necessarily mean the same choices for every community; one culture's idol is another culture's knick-knack. But Oriented Leaders remain vigilant in identifying those values and choices which compete with single minded commitment. Over time, compromise with distractions can become a cause for destruction. A track-record of faithfulness does not inoculate a community from future bankruptcy.

This is why Joshua was adamant. When the people spoke their wholehearted commitment to YHWH, they confirmed their vow. But the proof of their conviction was in their willingness to "throw away foreign gods".

Discussion Questions:

1) What are your congregation's current assets?
2) How are they calculated?
3) How is the value of those assets conveyed to the congregation?
4) What are the assets of your members?
5) How does membership in a congregation shift your priorities?
6) What choices do you make that demonstrate your priorities?
7) What choices do you make that conflict with your values?
8) Who inspects your choices to confirm your values?
9) For what cause would your congregation consider going into debt?
10) What would your congregation do differently if risk were not a concern?

CHAPTER 7

Document the Decision

And the people said to Joshua, "We will serve the LORD our God and obey him."

On that day Joshua made a covenant for the people, and there at Shechem he drew up for them decrees and laws. And Joshua recorded these things in the Book of the Law of God. Then he took a large stone and set it up there under the oak near the holy place of the LORD.

"See!" he said to all the people. "This stone will be a witness against us. It has heard all the words the LORD has said to us. It will be a witness against you if you are untrue to your God." [Joshua 24:24-27]

There are a whole bunch of rocks scattered throughout Joshua's Promised Land.

- Crossing Boulders on the west of the Jordan (Joshua 4)
- Execution Stones in the valley of Acor (Joshua 7)
- Altar of Renewal on Mt. Ebal (Joshua 8)
- Burial Rocks covering the cave of the Amorite kings (Joshua 10)
- Surveying Markers throughout the land (Joshua 13-17)
- A Witness Pillar at Shechem (Joshua 24)

Record-keeping was one of Joshua's passions.

For an Oriented Leader, careful documentation is not about recording victory, but settling disputes. Joshua believed formal documented reminders were important because they would prevent conflict, demonstrate fairness, and avoid pointless arguments concerning issues already discussed. For all of his strength in war Joshua's greater strength was demonstrated in how he documented peace.

Throughout his career as a leader, Joshua's systematic administration included three types of interrelated documentation: accounting, contract, and public notice. Each is of utmost importance for effective leadership.

Documented Accounting

Chapters 13-22 of the book of Joshua, provides a complete survey registrations of the land, a distribution which, as will be mentioned later, concentrates on fairness. The point of careful accounting is accountability.

Careful accounting is often dismissed as so much busy work, but conscientious recordkeeping provides a reviewable means to ensure integrity. It also settles disputes before they arise.

The most obvious congregational accounting is the recording of financial contribution and expenditure. As with all issues of integrity, leadership within every congregation should ensure a level of reporting consistent with the congregation's polity. Any attempt to thwart consistency opens leaders to accusations of mismanagement—or worse.

Congregational polity indicates the level of disclosure. A representative polity would require full financial transparency to the duly elected council or board. An Episcopal polity would require open records for examination by the hierarchy. Congregational polity would require full financial disclosure to every active member. Regardless of the polity, documentation confirms accountability by not only keeping leaders honest, but also by keeping their constituency informed.

Documented accessible accounting is necessary for leaders to competently make decisions. Without a shared understanding of a congregation's financial position reasonable risk cannot be assessed and unreasonable caution cannot be overturned. Insecure leaders frequently limit access to financial information in order to inflict their caution or hide their recklessness.

Accounting also includes careful documentation of the decision making process. Cataloguing the roll call of tribes every time Joshua addressed the people seems painfully redundant to the reader, but maintaining a record of attendance keeps participants accountable when they claim they were not included or informed.

Too often the accounting of process is ignored when things are "running smoothly". If people are in agreement, goes the thinking, why bother with the details of procedure? Theologically, however, congregations should bother with their decision-making process because God's presence and guidance is as important in times of ease as it is in times of stress. The Hebrew prophets frequently point out that the fall of the nation occurred, not when the cities were under siege, but when the people were wealthy and at peace. Their failure to adhere to due process in those times created the weakness later exploited by their enemies.

If, as I stated in Chapter 2 of Part I, polity is the expression of how God's Spirit is discerned by the community, then the minutes of a meeting are the record of how God's people have listened to the Spirit. Likewise, constitutions and bylaws are the rules of engagement between the people and the Spirit.

If, as Albert Einstein suggested, *God is in the details*, then it is in these recorded details God's Spirit lives and breathes through the community. Few among us are excited to sit down with congregational bylaws and the minutes of board meetings ready to review them for their dynamic prose. But the language of these documents conveys the community's "best guess" for spiritual discernment. The meeting's secretary is no less than the scribe for the Spirit's voice.

While consulting with various churches, I have found that a simple request for bylaws has turned into a lengthy search through file cabinets and boxes of material that have not been opened since the last major congregational conflict. This simple request raises all kinds of memories and pains of past conflicts and the assumption that I have made the request because I have discerned trouble. People are suspicious of formal process because these mechanisms of decision-making are usually consulted only when the conversation is divisive or cliques search for loopholes to circumvent power.

Not surprisingly, in the instances when formal process has fallen into disuse, congregational leadership has been poorly trained and more often than not, deeply entrenched among a small rotating circle of exhausted "faithful". New leaders, let alone new members, are not aware of how decisions are made, and the process of discernment degenerates into a set of informal conversations among individuals who embody institutional memory, occasionally referred to as the "old-guard".

Communities who have lost the explicit skill of recorded process find it difficult, even impossible, to effect change. Occasionally they can adopt new programs or add special events; but change without a record for orderly discernment is experienced as chaos.

The records of institutional process provide a framework within which transformation can occur. Any change will create discomfort; but when change is undertaken without a recorded process, the organization is open to sabotage.

Key issues in understanding the role of minutes and constitutional documents are principles of consistency and integrity. Failure to integrate theology and process creates an atmosphere of inconsistency that will, in times of conflict, undermine direction. Effective accounting articulates both how decisions are to be made, and how the process connects to underling ideals concerning the discernment of the Spirit.

This is why so many gatherings begin and end with prayer, not to invoke God's presence, but to inspire the attention of the participants to the discernment of God's voice.

Documented Contracts

Joshua understood the people's relationship with YHWH as contractual. In fact, the whole notion of a Covenant relationship was based upon the "if/then" language of contracts. Following the destruction of Ai in chapter 8, Joshua read the law to the people again on Mount Ebal. There he confirmed the contract by the construction of an altar witnessing their earnest-payment sacrifices to remain in relationship to their God.

Joshua drafted a formal treaty with the Gibeonites and required an oath signature by both parties (Joshua 9:14), and while the treaty was based on deception, Joshua insisted upon its enforcement because the people had given their word. Accountable relationships are made possible by clear contracts.

Again, in times of relative calm, it is tempting for congregations to rely upon informal agreements and casual commitments, but leaders who do not put things in writing have no assurance of enforcement once disagreement occurs. Embarrassed by unmet expectations, leadership is often left holding the bag of un-kept promises.

Trust is an important element of every interdependent relationship, but trust cannot exist where there is not a documented understanding of expectations.

The most common complaint from congregational volunteers is how they feel overworked. Their exhaustion arises from poor documentation. They commit to one task only to find they are expected to do a great deal more. Clearly delineated job descriptions for volunteer and staff prevent resentment, as people sign-on only for responsibilities they know in advance. Contracts also clarify the scope of projects so leadership knows how big the workforce needs to be in order to accomplish the task.

Job descriptions and documented contracts also allow the work to be transferrable. New members can more readily move into positions of responsibility if there is clarity regarding policies, procedures, and responsibilities.

After several years of trying to recruit volunteers for various activities, I learned that clearly delineated job descriptions together with public sign-up sheets yielded the best response. Each and every volunteer knew exactly what would be expected of him or her, and they saw how their job fit into the larger project. The public commitment reduced the number of individuals who said they would arrive but failed to show. The sign-up sheet provided the enforcement of public scrutiny.

Documented Public Notices

The relationship between contract and notice was also understood by Joshua. In the 24th chapter the children of Israel were renewing their contract with YHWH. Joshua understood the importance of public notice by erecting a witness pillar at Shechem.

Joshua had erected several public markers indicating moments of renewed commitment. The burial stones over the body of Achan were reminders to anyone who attempted to defy the commands of public finance. Likewise the stones sealing the tomb of the Amorite Kings marked the destiny for those who raised a sword against the Israelites.

Unfortunately, as every congregational leader knows, people do not always pay attention to the notices. The announcement can be made from the pulpit, printed in the newsletter, included in the Sunday bulletin, placed on flyers throughout the building, and there will be those who say they were not informed. The effectiveness of public notice cannot be measured by the members' response. People must be trained to interpret what the notices mean, and in providing the interpretation, they reinforce the message for themselves.

When small children saw the pile of stones in the valley of Achor (which means *valley of trouble*) it was up to the elders to tell again the story of Jericho, Ai, and the sin of Achan. When foreigners arrived at Shechem, it was up to the locals to interpret the meaning of the great pillar of witness. In telling the stories triggered by the public notice, those who hear the story learn their meaning, and those who tell the story are reminded of their message.

One congregation I served had a team of guides whose job it was to introduce every visitor to memorial plaques and bulletin boards. One of these guides told me he stopped missing meetings when he was forced to look at the notices every week. He also understood the history of his own congregation better and felt a deep sense of connection to its founders.

Over time public notices can be easily overlooked if leaders are not committed to pointing consistently to their meaning.

Documentation is not esoterica; it is the record of God's faithfulness, the people's commitment and direction.

Discussion Questions:

1) Who is responsible for keeping minutes for your meetings?
2) How is that information distributed? Is it read before the meeting?
3) Where are your constitution and/or bylaws? Have you read them?
4) Does your congregation have job descriptions for officers and volunteers?
5) Where are the records of your congregation's commitments? What are they?
6) Are there posters, plaques, or notices you do not understand? Do you know who could interpret them for you?
7) Could a brand new visitor know where and when relevant gatherings are held?
8) When have you volunteered for something only to find out your expectations do not match the need?
9) As a leader, are your expectations clear enough to document before you ask for volunteers?
10) What reminders of your commitments do you leave for others to interpret?

CHAPTER 8

Fairly Distribute Benefits

"Then Joshua sent the people away, each to his own inheritance." [Joshua 24:28]

T he bulk of the book of Joshua is really quite boring, as fairness usually is. Beginning with the list of defeated kings in chapter 12 and running through the allotment of cities for the Levites in chapter 21, the text is nothing more than a series of real estate surveys setting the property lines between tribes. It's not the stuff of great sermons, but it is the stuff of great administration.

Allotments outlined in the middle of the book demonstrate Joshua's commitment to fairness. While the eleven tribes[11] did not receive equal acreage, their inheritance is of comparable value. Each tribe received a set of major cities and surrounding villages together with sufficient farm and pasture land to sustain the infrastructure of their tribal district. So detailed is Joshua's account that the locations and boundaries have been little disputed by archeologists for centuries.

The tedium of fairness is one of the reasons why those in charge frequently drop the ball when faced with the task of giving credit. It is not only an issue of documentation, it is also the necessary research and analysis that calculates and defends reasonable outcomes for all who participate in the hard work of victory.

---

[11]   The tribe of Levi received no territory but instead was allotted a series of cities scattered throughout the nation (Joshua 21).

Giving credit where credit is due seldom lapses by intent; unfair distribution and poor recognition usually demonstrates a lack of diligence.[12]

Fairness makes commitment stronger

The primary difficulty for leaders is follow-through. How the rewards are distributed tends to be considered somewhere towards the end of a project when there are actually rewards. But what both Moses and Joshua understood was how a clear guide to distribution must be conveyed from the beginning. Joshua allocated some lands before the region was completely conquered (Joshua 13:2-7). Knowing the benefits before the battle made the fighting even stronger.

One sizable suburban congregation was experiencing a generational change in its leadership. Several board members in their eighties were stepping down to make way for leadership less than half their age. Consulting with the leadership as to why the transition seemed to be going so smoothly, one outgoing elder told me, "[The new leadership] is going to take really good care of us!"

It's easier to share when you know that you're going to be included.

Fairness requires negotiation

In Joshua 17, representatives of Ephraim and Manasseh were concerned because it appeared their region would be insufficient to support their population.

> The people of Joseph said to Joshua, "Why have you given us only one allotment and one portion for an inheritance? We are a numerous people and the LORD has blessed us abundantly."
>
> "If you are so numerous," Joshua answered, "and if the hill country of Ephraim is too small for you, go up into the forest and clear land for yourselves there in the land of the Perizzites and Rephaites."

---

[12] I am reminded of the theme song of Gilligan's Island where each character is named until the end of the song which merely states, "And the rest!" when there were only two more characters to include. The song had been written before the cast list had been set. The theme song had to be changed for the second and subsequent seasons after contract negotiations with Russell Johnson and Dawn Wells.

> The people of Joseph replied, "The hill country is not enough for us, and all the Canaanites who live in the plain have iron chariots, both those in Beth Shan and its settlements and those in the Valley of Jezreel."
>
> But Joshua said to the house of Joseph—to Ephraim and Manasseh—"You are numerous and very powerful. You will have not only one allotment but the forested hill country as well. Clear it, and its farthest limits will be yours; though the Canaanites have iron chariots and though they are strong, you can drive them out." (Joshua 17:14-18)

Joshua acknowledges the validity of the tribe's concern, but he was unwilling to allow the tribes to cut territory from other allotments. If Ephraim and Manasseh needed more space, they would need to participate in their own expansion. While adjusting the compensation to fit the need, Joshua made the people responsible for insuring the outcome.

Routinely congregational resources are allocated as competing priorities. Sunday school teachers argue with literacy tutors over the use of rooms and chalk, the bell-choir argues with the children's choir over rehearsal time, the early service coffee fellowship is too noisy for the adult study group, and everybody wants to use the kitchen but nobody wants to clean it. Leaders should always keep in mind these are happy problems. When scarcity is created by shared need Oriented Leaders see opportunity for expansion.

Turning the issue from competition to capacity, Joshua increased the total resources available for the Israelites. Joshua affirmed not only the need, but also their capacity to meet their need.

Fairness requires transparency

From the beginning the leaders' pay was published.

> Then Joshua blessed Caleb son of Jephunneh and gave him Hebron as his inheritance. So Hebron has belonged to Caleb son of Jephunneh the Kenizzite ever since, because he followed the LORD, the God of Israel, wholeheartedly. (Joshua 14:13-14)
>
> When they had finished dividing the land into its allotted portions, the Israelites gave Joshua son of Nun an

inheritance among them, as the LORD had commanded. They gave him the town he asked for—Timnath Serah in the hill country of Ephraim. And he built up the town and settled there. (Joshua 19:49-50)

I have seen annual reports where pastoral compensation in large multi-staff congregations is lumped into a single line-item. I have consulted in congregations where only the treasurer and one or two trustees know the pastor's salary. I have seen the pastor's housing-allowance tucked into the budget for building maintenance, and I have known several clergy who have co-mingled congregational expenses with personal purchases. And in every instance people have made remarks.

Credibility regarding stewardship, fairness, and financial disclosure, begins with reasonable disclosure regarding the leader's compensation.

When confronted with questions regarding disclosure of salary, housing, pension contributions, insurance, and expense allowances, pastors often respond, "We don't publish that because the people really wouldn't understand."

This raises two concerns for me. First, what are they trying to hide? Second, why would it be so difficult to explain?

There will always be those who dispute compensation. For many it is the only time they have the opportunity to participate in such a discussion and usually debates over the pastor's salary arise from other issues.

A friend of mine who had served as assistant-pastor of a large urban congregation took a call to a small-town congregation. Moving from complete dependence on public transportation to a place where half of his congregation lived in the country meant he would have to purchase a vehicle. I took him car shopping. After considering several models in his price range he settled on a non-descript, mid-priced, four-door sedan. "It is," he said, "the perfect pastor's car. It is in every way unremarkable."

Fairness creates long-term stability

For dozens of generations the children of Israel lived within their tribal states without debate. This was partially due to Joshua's meticulous record keeping and surveying, but the endurance of the property lines was made possible by their fairness.

Providing for fairness from the beginning of the project allows participants to see their value. Each tribe's reward was prepared prior to their commitment, and the preparation ensured reward in proportion to their need.

Too often in congregations, recognition and reward are determined by the sensitivity of the recognized individuals or group. Leaders are tempted to placate whiners by making a big deal over their meager contributions, ignoring more substantial gifts provided by the modest. Such treatment, while expedient, is poor training for the congregation's future. Those standing on the sidelines considering their contribution quickly learn that honor is bestowed upon the complainers not the generous.

Some individuals may not require public praise for their efforts, in fact the most mature seldom do. The issue is not individual praise but corporate accountability.

Joshua did not allocate the land based upon the complaints of the tribes, but upon their legitimate corporate needs. Oriented Leaders remember that the needs of the community are not defined by what they *hear*, but by what they honestly *witness*.

Fair distribution of benefits is not only the conclusion of every successful campaign, but also the foundation for future participation.

Discussion Questions:

1) What are the rewards of being a part of your congregation?
2) How are those rewards divided?
3) Do you clearly define success before each project?
4) Have there been times when you've felt you were dismissed and others were honored?
5) Who is responsible for recognizing member's contributions?
6) Do your leaders know what gifts you bring or is that information strictly confidential?
7) Are financial commitments confidential but contributions of time or expertise public?
8) Do you know your pastor(s) salary? Should you?
9) Are there those in your congregation who receive too much attention? Are there those who receive too little?
10) Can visitors to your congregation recognize the fairness with which participants are treated? Why or why not?

CONCLUSION

From Wilderness Wandering
to Promise Dwelling

It seems obvious but Oriented Leadership must begin where you are. Envisioning some wondrous future can be exhilarating, but often, as the old New Englander saying goes, "You can't get there from here." More importantly, however, you can't get anywhere if you don't start from here. Yet knowing exactly *where* you are isn't easy.

When the book of Joshua opens, they are on the east side of the Jordan River. They've been there for over 39 years. Three days later, they're on the west side of the Jordan River, a move of only a few hundred feet. The children of Israel moved a short geographic distance, but they traversed a significant spiritual distance—they moved from possibility to promise.

Once across the Jordan the soles of their feet made contact with the longing of their souls. On the west side of the river they stood, quite literally, on the evidence of the fulfilled Covenant.

This was the land God had promised centuries before to Abraham, Isaac, and Jacob. This was the move they had anticipated with their parents and grandparents when they crossed the Red Sea four decades before. This was the generation who would live into the promise.

To determine where you are starting, Oriented Leadership must ask, "On which side of the Jordan River are the people standing?"

For the Christian community this is a question of theological geography. It is a question regarding the orientation of Christian baptism.

Traditionally the baptismal debates of the Church regard technique. Some congregations believe authentic baptism must be chosen. Baptismal candidates

---

169

must wait until they reach maturity—an age of accountability. At that time baptism confirms a personal and cognitively understood confession of faith witnessed by the congregation who affirms one's right to be baptized. This tradition is known as "believer's baptism", a rite reserved for those who make a personal and public confession to follow the Lord in the waters baptism.

Believer's baptism highlights the importance of individual conversion, and usually insists the baptismal candidate be immersed—that is put under the water until they bubble.

Sometimes these baptismal services are held near a natural body of water like a river, lake, or stream. This setting is familiar to me as I grew up with tent-meetings followed by baptismal services at Carter Lake, or Lake Okoboji. The morning following an evangelistic service altar-call, the congregation would gather at the lake-front to baptize those who were *saved* the night before. The service opened with a hymn followed by time for testimonies. The pastor or evangelist stepped into the water and plunged the sinners beneath the surface with the declaration they had died to the sins of this world and risen with Christ to eternal life.

Sometimes believer's baptism takes place in a pool inside a sanctuary filled deep with water. That is how I was baptized as a 13 year-old at the Omaha Gospel Tabernacle in a Sunday evening service in August, 1974 by the Reverend Albert Runge. Stepping down into a pool behind the choir-loft I was immersed and welcomed as a member of the congregation and as one received into the family of God. (I was startled to see the pastor in hip-waders, somehow it didn't seem fair; but it did explain how it only took one hymn for him to dry off between the last baptism and his re-appearance in the pulpit for the sermon.)

A majority of Christians were baptized at a time they cannot recall. As infants they were brought by their family to the font with God-parents, sponsors, or guardians. There the minister or priest declared the child's welcome to the community of faith. On behalf of the baptized, grown-ups agreed to raise the child in the "nurture and admonition of the Lord", which has something to do with spanking and Sunday school.

Perhaps there was a party after the event; infants don't remember. But someone thought it important enough to bring the child into the community of the faithful. There, God's love was proclaimed when they were still filling their pants. For many who were baptized as children, the vows were personally appropriated years later when they stood before the congregation in the rite or sacrament of confirmation.

Regardless of the form, baptism is a profound declaration; simple life-sustaining water identifies God's own. The waters of baptism are not magical. I do not believe the disposition of one's soul rests upon the presence or absence of droplets spread in the right quantity mixed with special words. God's disposition does not shift merely because one has or has not received the proper ordinance, rite, or sacrament. The value of baptism is not what God says about us, but what the community of faith proclaims regarding those whom they have baptized. It is an audacious declaration;

> **Behold, what manner of love the Father hath bestowed upon us, that we should be called the [children] of God.**
> **(I John 1:3a)**

The act of baptism is available not because we are saved, but because we are fallen. Each and every baptismal candidate comes to the font, the shore, or the pool precisely because he or she needs to break from the snares of this world and live in the orientation of God's promise.

A friend of mine startles his otherwise staid Presbyterian congregation by beckoning the parents to present their infants for baptism with the call, "Bring the little sinners to the font!"

The traditional questions regarding baptism's administrative form become trivial when compared to the deeper question regarding the theological geography of baptism. For Oriented Leaders the question is not *"How* were you baptized?" or *"When* should one be baptized?" But *"Whither* do the members of your community stand, once they have been baptized?"

Regardless of location or requirements, whether an adult candidate stands in the muddy stagnate water of a fishing-hole made sacred for the morning, or an infant is carried to a marble-hewn font crafted for the sacrament, whether the water rushed by in the current of a mountain stream or was poured from a crystal cruet, baptism declares to all creation that these men and women, boys and girls, are set apart from the lies of this world to bask in the refreshing purifying knowledge of God's eternal grace.

The question of baptismal movement does not reference architecture or plumbing; it's not even a concern over language or liturgy. The question regards the *theological movement.* Where do we believe our baptism has taken us? The answer to this question orients every step the people of God take following their baptism.

Baptismal movement orients the heart, life, actions, and attitudes of the congregation. Orienting baptism is important because while there are two major traditions regarding the form of baptism—"infant" and "believers"—there are also two traditions regarding the movement of baptism.

Hebrew Scripture references two great water movements for the children of Israel. The first brought them out of Egypt (Exodus 13); the Red Sea parted and the children of Israel were delivered from slavery as the enemy was swallowed-up. These waters were evidence of their freedom from bondage, but not their deliverance into the Land of Promise. The waters of the Red Sea moved the community from captivity to wilderness.

The second baptismal movement in Hebrew Scripture was the crossing of the Jordan, when the people came into the Promised Land (Joshua 3). There they were delivered from the wilderness into the unfolding reality of a fulfilled Covenant.

How leaders orient their congregations is a baptismal question. Are they baptized in the Red Sea, moving from bondage to wilderness? Or are they baptized in the Jordan moving from desert wandering to promise dwelling?

I believe faithful dynamic congregations have crossed the Jordan; they are orientated to dwell in the realized realm of God's Covenant. They plan, live, work, function, minister, and play not as shadowy desert dwellers, but as inheritors of a graciously fulfilled promise.

The leaders of healthy congregations do not see their communities as children wandering in insufficiency, but rather greet their companions as gifted citizens of the Covenant. This orientation, to live on the *other* side of the Jordan, transforms everything!

Most of my disappointments, frustrations, and personal "demons" arise when I live believing I am stuck in the wilderness, failing to recognize I am dwelling in the Promise. When I believe myself to be in the wilderness, every setback is one more example of how incomplete my life must be—how tragically short my resources!

But when I look around and determine that this is the place God has prepared for me, this is the time in which God is present—the promise has been fulfilled—then day-to-day difficulties are nothing less than opportunities to discover how God supplies what my life requires.

It startles me every time I read the opening words of the book of Joshua. Forty years in the wilderness, forty years with only two and one half tribes "home". Three days and they moved!

The space where they dwelled for 39 ½ years they conquered back in Exodus 17. All that time Joshua was commander of the army, but his command did not include the authority to lead. Joshua defeated the Amorites; the land east of the Jordan was claimed just a few short months after they left Egypt. They started on their journey crossing the Red Sea, claiming a tiny part of their territory and then, sat down. Twelve tribes camped-out for nearly four decades on a piece of territory intended for two and one-half tribes. The Reubenites, Gadites, and half of the tribe of Manasseh were home, but the remaining nine and one-half tribes were squatting with relatives. There a commander without authority waited too.

Like middle-aged children still living in their parent's basement, the remaining nine and one-half tribes set up housekeeping in the wilderness when the Land of Promise was a river-walk away. For nearly four decades it seemed to be okay.

All that time, only one more push and they would have been home. Across the river they could see their land—a dwelling-place they could call their own—if only they had listened to Joshua and Caleb! They were so close to success, but wilderness-thinking sabotaged their movement.

Wilderness-thinkers are complacent with insufficiency. They believe it is reasonable to live with only a portion of the promise. Rather than finish the task to which they were created to accomplish, wilderness-thinkers imagine that the risks are too great, the giants too formidable, and the cost too high. They postpone Covenant-living for another time, perhaps *"whenna we die"*.

Wilderness-thinking develops its own "spiritualized" justification which paralyzes courage and stagnates movement. Wilderness-thinking justifies things the way they are because they are better than they were. Wilderness dwellers just *camp-out* with "good enough" and never *step-out* to discover what's beyond the river.

Wilderness congregations grow, flourish, press forward, arrive at a plateau and there they get stuck. They hunker down in the wilderness—where things are better than they *were*, but not what they *could be*. Occasionally, they call in a consultant, but with the caveats, "You have to understand resources are scarce, our congregation is getting older, we don't have the young people like we used to, the neighborhood has changed, we don't have the money, we're just here in the wilderness waiting, being faithful, leaving the promise for somebody else."

Wilderness spirituality can be very seductive. After all, some of the best songs are written for those dwelling on the wilderness side of the Jordan.

> I looked cross Jordan and what did I see?
> Coming for to carry me home!
> A band of angels coming after me!
> Coming for to carry me home.[13]

> Or

> Deep river, my home is over Jordan.
> Deep river, Lord, I wanna cross over into camp ground.

> All God's children, oh don't you wanna go
> to the heavenly feast
> in that Promised Land where all is peace?

---

[13] "Swing Low, Sweet Chariot" was composed by Wallis Willis, a Choctaw freedman in the old Indian Territory, sometime before 1862.

Walk right into Heaven and take my seat
and throw myself at Jesus' feet.[14]

Or

My Lord knows the way through the wilderness,
all we have to do is follow.[15]

And when wilderness congregations get through one crisis they circle back to where they were before because, "My Lord knows the way through the wilderness, all we have to do is follow," then they circle back around to where they were before because, "My Lord knows the way . . . ."

Wilderness leaders coach the people to proceed carefully, cautiously, even piously, but the only thing the congregation learns is how to stay in the wilderness because that is where their leadership has oriented them to be.

In baptism, however, God does not call us into the wilderness. God calls us *through* the wilderness. At baptism we proclaim our inheritance; we grasp the reality of the Promise.

The Exodus had a purpose; it was moving the people out so the people could move home. Far too many congregations do not claim the river Jordan as the locus of their baptism, it is as if their baptism was through the Red Sea, and the Jordan is reserved only as a metaphor for death.

I stood on the river of Jordan
to see that ship come sailing over.
Stood on the river of Jordan,
O see that ship sail by!

O mourner, don't you weep,
when you see that ship come sailing over
Shout, "Glory, Hallelujah!"
when you see that ship sail by.[16]

---

[14] "Deep River" is an anonymous spiritual of African-American origin.
[15] Sidney Cox, ©1951
[16] "I Stood on the River of Jordan" is an anonymous spiritual of African-American origin.

Historically, the tradition of the wilderness spiritual arose from the helplessness of Negro slaves. Slaves existed in constant dependence on the whim of their owners; life was filled with nothing more than trial and sorrow. These songs expressed how the sweat, temptation, and shortages of this world were nothing more than a contrast to glorious eternal life, yet to come. In this wilderness the best one could do was to dream for a better place, because each day's sustenance came by God's grace not by self-determined possibility. On this wilderness side of the Jordan, one could only hope for a little manna.

Slavery begat images of life-eternal, an unseen land flowing with milk and honey. The only conceivable way to experience the evidence of God's promise was to cross the Jordan through death.

The scriptural image of wilderness-dwelling can faithfully be applied in times of powerful depravation, when life *truly* languishes in the desert. Abandonment, scarcity, loss, tragedy, helplessness, all can evoke spiritual resonance with the stories and songs of a people longing for home. But faithful leadership, oriented in present reality, needs to honestly appraise the surroundings to determine if wilderness thinking authentically applies.

Much of the wilderness experience seems apropos when leaders face opposition. But so compelling is the story of the Exodus that organizations often invent crises to identify with a God of liberation rather than a God of expectation.

This situation describes many American Christian Congregations. Way beyond church planting days, congregations hunker down in paid-off facilities, with savings, curriculums, directories, and websites, only to bemoan their "wilderness" status. Absent any real challenge, they trump up the powers of secular culture, or declining attendance, or unmet budgets, and immediately identify with the wandering children of Israel longing for a "better" homeland.

Faced with an opportunity for outreach, mission, or fellowship, they immediately respond as the Israelites did at Kadesh, rending their garments and planning defection. Among them there may be "Joshuas" who call the people to identity and purpose, but without granting them the authority, the congregation remains stuck. Missing is the prophetic word which insists on movement into promise, and believes movement is the reason for struggle. Missing is the reminder of God's identification not with a people enslaved or wandering, but with a people moving into the fullness of their identity.

Absent such leaders the people perish as they wander without direction, without reason, without spirit.

Most American congregations in this day and age are not in the wilderness; they are, in fact, residents of a Promised Land, surrounded by the fulfillment of God's promise to provide.

As men, women, boys, and girls are baptized into the community of faith, the Good News is, we are *already* home. We are already citizens of the Covenant and baptism is the river-walk that moves God's people from wandering hope to settled promise.

For congregational leaders the issue is simply location, your people have long crossed the Red Sea it's time to end their wandering; baptism was through the Jordan, and now it is time to live in the promise.

This simple movement transforms the possibilities of a people. In Joshua 1 Moses had been dead for only thirty days. The children mourned his death, they missed their beloved liberator and law giver; but when the time for mourning ended, the entire orientation of the people changed.

Joshua refused to coddle a wilderness congregation; he chose instead to command a Covenant people. Joshua's inaugural address was simple; you've got three days to move on. After two score years of sitting around, after four decades of going nowhere, after forty years of feeling sorry for themselves, the people of the wilderness picked-up and moved into the Promised Land.

What changed? Same army, same supplies, same enemy, same river, the change was leadership. And so in fewer days than they had been stuck years—they were in the Land of Promise.

It is the baptismal point made by John the Baptist.

> In those days John the Baptist came, preaching in the Desert of Judea and saying, "Repent, for the kingdom of heaven is near." This is he who was spoken of through the prophet Isaiah: "A voice of one calling in the desert, 'Prepare the way for the Lord, make straight paths for him.'"

> John's clothes were made of camel's hair, and he had a leather belt around his waist. His food was locusts and wild honey. People went out to him from Jerusalem and all Judea and the whole region of the Jordan. Confessing their sins, they were baptized by him in the Jordan River. (Matthew 3:1-6)

> And what did John say of himself?

> "'I baptize you with water for repentance.'"

John's baptism declared what happened at the Red Sea—freedom from slavery, from bondage, from the captivity to this fallen world. But he pointed to another movement beyond those waters.

> **. . . after me will come one who is more powerful than I, whose sandals I am not fit to carry. He will baptize you with the Holy Spirit and with fire. (Matthew 3:11)**

John identified Jesus as the one whose baptism moved us from the wilderness call of redundant repentance, to the Promised Land of Covenant dwelling.

"But wait!" the congregation will cry. "This can't be the Promised Land, we've got bills! We've got uncooperative members; our youth program is struggling; there are building repairs! How can this be the Promised Land?"

In the orientation of the Promised Land leaders must remember, that there is no more manna (Joshua 5:12). In the years to come the children of Israel learned the only food they would eat, was the food they would plant. In the Promised Land, building houses was more difficult than pitching tents; figuring out how to get along with neighbors was more complicated than moving camp. Promised Land living isn't easy; even after the conquest the children of Israel had to work.

Living in the Promised Land does not mean we cease to struggle, it simply means we are home. We are in the place God wants us to be.

To be oriented trans-Jordan does not change the amount of work to be done, it transforms the interpretation of that work. It does not shift the barriers to progress, it merely leaves the removal of those barriers to the work we are willing to do. Oriented Leaders must fit the people to live in the land of promise, because there is one more chilling lesson from the Hebrew Scriptures, one the children of Israel learned generations later from the prophet Jeremiah—the Promised Land can be lost!

This is the warning to congregational leaders in this time and place. We either challenge our people to do the hard work of building on God's realized promise, or we will lose the bounty of our inheritance.

Without vision the people *will* perish!

What's more, in that same proverb, the Hebrew word for *perish* literally means to become scattered around like garbage on the street, or unrestrained like animals broken out of their pens.

Without the ability to see the people clearly, *as* they are and *who* they are, the congregation becomes like stuff scattered around or animals wandering off. Leaders with an oriented vision allow the people to be restrained, uncluttered, organized—administered.

As Christians our scripture, theology, and tradition speak volumes about who these people *really* are. They are children of God, called, redeemed, loved, and given the Holy Spirit for the work of the Church. If leaders do not keep this clear vision, then whole congregations become a scattered, wandering mess.

Church leaders need vision, a clarity that sees through the dark glass of human condition and envisions the people as they truly are and must continue to be—the living, breathing expressions of God's promise, and collectively, Christ's body.

The buildings, the endowments, programs, steeples, pews, stained-glass, the education wings, parking-lots, pulpits, and most tragically, the people themselves will become the possession of another if we fail to live as God has called us—if we fail to learn the leadership principles of the ancient warrior, Joshua.

INDEX

Get Published, Inc!
Thorofare, NJ 08086
25 August 2009
BA2009237